HORSE
ILLUSTRATED TRAINING **GUIDE**

Caring
for Your Horse

Written and Photographed by Lesley Ward

A Division of BowTie, Inc.
Irvine, California

Roger Sipe, *Special Projects Editor*
Lindsay Hanks, *Associate Editor*
Matt Hennings, *Art Director*
Jessica Jaensch, *Production Coordinator*
June Kikuchi, Andrew DePrisco, *Editorial Directors*

The horses in this book are referred to as he or she in alternating chapters unless their gender is apparent from the activity discussed.

Library of Congress Cataloging-in-Publication Data

Ward, Lesley.
  Caring for your horse / by Lesley Ward.
      p. cm.
  "Previously published as "Horse illustrated guide to caring for your horse" by Lesley Ward.
  Includes bibliographical references.
  ISBN 978-1-935484-51-6
  1. Horses. I. Ward, Lesley. Horse illustrated guide to caring for your horse. II. Title.

  SF285.3.W37 2010
  636.1'083--dc22
                        2010014069

BowTie Press®
A Division of BowTie, Inc.
3 Burroughs
Irvine, CA 92618
Printed and bound in the United States
14 13 12 11 10   1 2 3 4 5

acknowledgments

I would like to thank the following people for their help with this book:

Kim Abbott; Marian Abe; Sharon Biggs; Jane Butteriss; Marge Fritze;

Jane Frusher; Allison Griest; Paula Grimstead; Diane Harkey; Moira C. Harris;

Lon Hyers; Kelly James; Denise Justice; Eric Matthews; Julie Mignery; Carol Nelson;

Jennifer Nice; Sherry Pascual; Heather Hayes Schram; Jennifer Smith;

Annette Slowinski, D.V.M.; Katherine Waldrop; Holly Werner;

and finally, my father, Alan Ward, for his excellent editing skills.

Contents

Introduction

You've finally found the horse of your dreams. He's passed the vet exam, you've paid for him, and you've taken him home. Now the fun truly begins. Your new horse is going to need a lot of your time, and it is up to you to keep him healthy and happy. The way he looks and feels largely depends on the way you care for him, so you should do it right.

This book describes the basics of horse care and management: important information that every horse owner needs to know. You'll learn how to handle your horse and make his new home a comfortable and safe place. You'll also learn about grooming, feeding, and tacking up. This book is full of tips to keep your horse healthy and in tip-top shape. You'll know if your horse isn't feeling 100 percent and what to do if he gets injured.

Owning a horse is a major responsibility. Even if your horse is kept at a boarding facility and others do most of the work for you, it is in your best interest to know as much as you can about horse health and stable management.

Nobody truly cares about your horse or has your investment in his well-being as much as you do. Even at the best barns, illnesses are missed and injuries are overlooked. You need to be familiar with your horse from head to hoof.

Taking care of a horse can be a lot of work, but the rewards are great. A horse who is properly cared for has a lot of energy and is fun to ride. If he eats the right diet and is groomed on a regular basis, he'll look great and you'll be proud of him—whether competing at a show or simply walking him around the barn. Looking after a living, breathing, occasionally unpredictable 1,000-pound-plus animal can be a challenge at times, but this book will prepare you for the task.

Handling a Horse

*i*f you've been taking regular riding lessons, you already have had some handling experience. Handling describes the activities you do with a horse while on the ground such as catching him, leading him, and working around him.

It's very important to learn correct handling for your own safety. Horses can be unpredictable, and even the quietest, most sensible horse can spook and run off. When a horse is upset, he will step on you or knock you over without a thought because his instinct is to escape whatever is upsetting him. This is why you should always be aware when you're around a horse. Almost anything could happen.

Understanding Horse Behavior

Understanding horse behavior helps you know how to react if your horse acts badly or does something that seems strange. Here are a few things to consider:

Horses, by nature, are herd creatures. They like to be in the company of other horses. This behavior dates back thousands of years to when your horse's ancestors lived in the wild. It was much safer for them to live in a herd because a solitary horse was more likely to get attacked and eaten by a predator. Some horses are hard to catch when out in a field because they don't want to leave their herdmates. Similarly, if you are riding a horse in company, he may be reluctant to go away from his buddies.

Horses would rather run than fight. Their primary defense is running, which is why they spook or shy (jump or run away from scary objects) so much. If they spot something they think is dangerous, their natural reaction is to run away from it: a response that may have helped them survive for millions of years. Remember this when your horse reacts violently to a flapping garbage bag or an unusual noise. His first reaction may be to get away from it fast. Try not to punish this behavior, as it is only natural.

Horses take their cues from other horses. If one horse becomes antsy in the warm-up arena at a show for example, it is likely that others will catch on and act badly too. If one horse won't be caught in a field, others also may be difficult to catch.

Horses have remarkable memories. This can be good and bad. A good memory is a plus when you teach a horse a new task and he remembers it the next time. But if he has a bad experience, such as a terrible ride in a trailer or a painful visit with the veterinarian, he will remember it for years.

Horse Sense

A horse can smell things you can't, hear things you can't, and see things you can't. That's why he may react strongly to something you don't sense. He may be nervous because he can smell a coyote a mile down the trail, or he may spook at a child running behind you in the arena. It's important to know about the senses that keep a horse aware of what's going on around him.

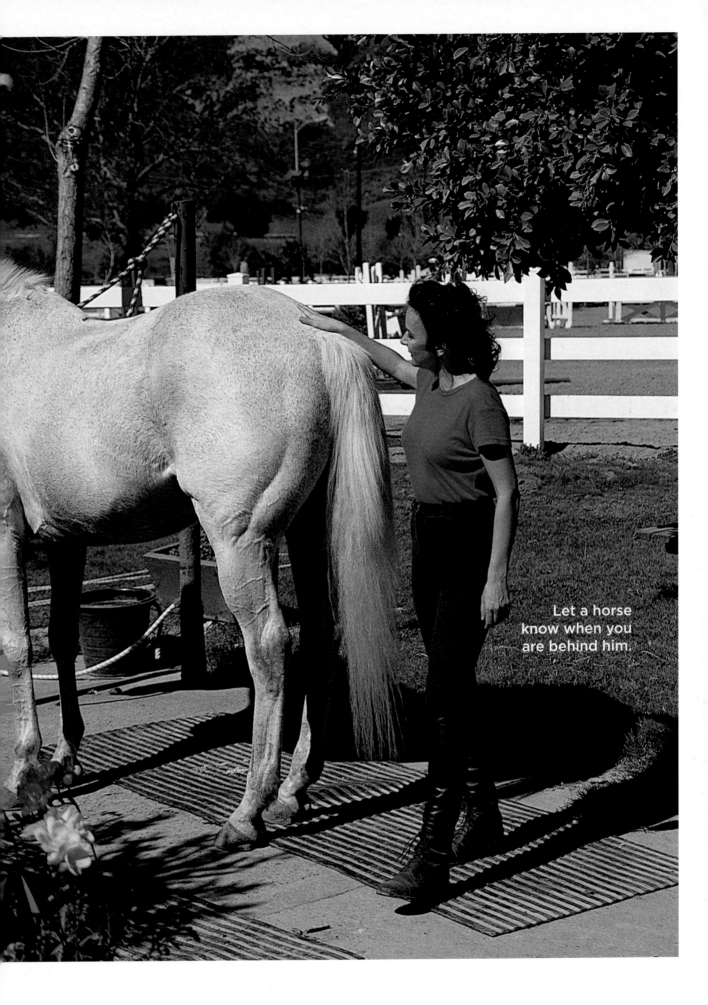

Let a horse
know when you
are behind him.

VISION

Horses have a unique way of seeing things. They have the largest eyes of any land mammal. The placement of their eyes on the sides of the head gives them a wide field of view—reportedly up to a radius of 200 degrees. Horses, however, don't see objects well directly in front or directly behind themselves, so keep that in mind when you are trail riding or riding in a new area. Horses do have night vision, but it is not as acute as a cat or a dog's. Once in darkness, a horse's night vision is impaired when light is briefly introduced.

Move carefully around the following areas:

- directly behind the tail

- directly in front of the forehead

- under his head and around the front legs

If you have to groom a horse around these areas, speak to the horse so he knows where you are.

HEARING

A horse has large, funnel-shaped ears that catch even the tiniest noise. They also rotate so the horse can hear sounds from any direction. If a horse hears something that interests him, both of his ears will point toward the source of the sound.

SMELL

When a horse spots something scary, once he feels brave enough, he'll give it a big sniff. If he meets a new horse, he'll sniff him, too, so that he can later identify the other horse as familiar and safe, or hostile and dangerous. Your horse will soon come to recognize your smell.

TOUCH

A horse's skin is very sensitive. Notice how he can flick away the tiniest fly, no matter where it lands on his body. Some horses hate being groomed with a hard brush and fidget and grind their teeth. Make your horse happy and use a soft brush. The areas around the nose and mouth are particularly sensitive, so avoid patting or touching him there. You might think stroking your horse's nose would be soothing, but he'd probably prefer that you pat him on the neck instead.

Horse "Talk"

A horse's body language can tell you what he's feeling and help you predict what he's going to do. You can avoid accidents by paying close attention to your horse's body language.

Here are some interpretations of common horse body language:

- Pinning his ears back means he feels angry or threatened.

- Pawing with his front hooves means he is impatient or hungry.

- Swishing his tail violently means he is irritated or grumpy.

- Swinging his hindquarters toward you means he's afraid of you or he may kick.

- Lifting a leg could mean he is preparing to kick.

- Ears forward, head reaching toward you means he's interested in you. He may be asking, "Hey, do you have a treat for me?"

- Resting a hind leg could mean he is tired or simply feeling relaxed.

Stand on your horse's near side when catching him.

When a horse points his ears, something has interested him.

Catching a Horse

If your horse spends most of his time in a field or corral, you'll have to catch him before you can ride him. This might be difficult because you should turn him out without a halter. Halters, especially tough nylon ones, can get caught on branches or fencing and seriously injure your horse. If your horse is hard to catch, turn him out in a leather halter; it will break if it gets caught on something.

If your horse is friendly, catching him shouldn't be difficult, especially if you have a tasty treat—such as an apple—in your pocket.

Here's the best way to catch a horse:

1 Carry a halter and a lead rope into the field. Close the gate behind you. Call to your horse so he knows you're approaching. Walk slowly, in

an indirect arc toward him. If he doesn't come, walk toward his side so he can see you clearly. Aim for his left shoulder so you'll be in the correct position to put on his halter quickly.

2 Stand on his near (left) side, next to his shoulder, and face the same direction he's facing. Give him a treat as a reward for coming to you or standing still, then slip the lead rope over his neck and hold the two parts of the rope together with one hand under his throat. This gives you some control so it is harder for your horse to escape.

3 Place the noseband of the halter over his nose, then pass the crownpiece behind his ears, and buckle it. Always give him a pat on the neck to let him know how good he is. Being caught should be a pleasant experience!

CATCH ME IF YOU CAN!

Some horses don't like to be caught, and there are few things more annoying than chasing a wily horse around a field for hours!

Here are some tricks that might help:

- Many horses associate being caught with working. Go out in the field occasionally just to visit your horse. Put on his halter, give him a treat, and then let him go.

- Carry the halter and lead rope behind your back so the horse can't see it.

- Most horses are greedy and investigate anything that sounds like food. If your horse is by himself in the field, carry a bucket with some feed and shake it. Put down the bucket, and he should put his head in it. Wrap the lead rope around his neck and, *voilà*, he's trapped. Never carry a bucket of feed into a field full of horses; they may fight over it, and you could get kicked and seriously injured.

- Horses are nosy. Carry a squeaky toy or a crumpled piece of paper and squeak or rustle it near your horse. If he comes over, move slowly so as not to frighten him off and cause him to bolt.

- Walk in a large circle around your horse, then slowly spiral in until you're close enough to put on his halter.

- If you're desperate, lead his field mates out of the field. Your horse will probably loiter around the gate, eager to be with them. When he is alone, he may be easier to catch.

Turning out a Horse

Carefully open the gate wide enough for you and your horse to walk through side by side. Once you're in the field, turn your horse around so he is facing the gate. Close the gate, take off his halter, and let him go. Don't let your horse loose when he is facing the field; the temptation for him might be too great. He might get frisky and try to run off, and you could get kicked and seriously injured or trampled. When in doubt, have a friend or trainer help you the first few times you turn out your horse. An extra hand is always helpful in case you lose control of the horse.

Leading a Horse in a Halter

Stand next to your horse's shoulder, facing the same direction that he's facing. (He should be on your right.) Clip the lead rope to the metal ring on the halter under his chin. Your right hand

A bucket
of food may
entice a hard-
to-catch horse.

should hold the lead rope about 3 inches under the chin. Loop the excess rope and hold the loops in the middle with your left hand. Don't wind it around your hand; if your horse runs off, you could be dragged behind him. Walk even to your horse's shoulder; don't get too far in front or behind.

To stop him, come to a complete halt and say "whoa." If he does not stop immediately, tug once or twice on the lead rope with your right hand and say "whoa" again.

Leading Problems

If your horse likes to drag you along and nibble every blade of grass, you may have to use a stud chain over his nose to keep his attention, similar to a choke chain on a dog. You can buy one at a tack store for a couple of dollars. Thread the snap end through the square bit of metal on the buckle (left) side of the halter, run it over the noseband, thread it through the square on the far side, and then snap it to the round ring halfway up his head. Then attach the lead rope to the chain at the bottom. Walk next to your horse normally, but tug on the lead rope if he tries to get away from you. This pulls on the chain, which puts pressure on his nose. He should listen to you pretty quickly, and after a few days you should be able to remove the chain.

If your horse is sluggish when you lead him, carry a long dressage whip—not to hit, but to use as an extension of your arm. This type of whip is best because it reaches his hindquarters, which is the prime tapping area. Hold the lead rope as usual, and carry the whip in your left hand. If your horse does not move forward when you ask, flick the whip sideways behind you and tap him on his hindquarters so he understands that you want him to move—now!

Hold the lead rope with two hands.

If your horse is a puller, you may need to put a chain over his nose.

As a safety precaution, tie the lead rope to a loop of safety twine.

Tying up a Horse

Always tie your horse in a safe place, with plenty of space between him and other horses. Always tie him in a halter. Never tie your horse with his reins; if he spooks, he will pull back, the bridle may break, and the bit will hurt his mouth.

Tie your horse to a specially mounted metal ring or a solid object such as a tree or fence post. Never tie him to anything that isn't firmly planted in the ground that he could run away

with—even something heavy like a picnic table. As a safety precaution, tie a loop of safety string (usually baling twine) first and then attach the lead rope to the string. If your horse pulls back, he will break the string instead of his lead rope, his halter, or even his neck.

Tie him up high and fairly short, so he can't trip over the lead rope. About 18 inches from the ring or post is adequate. And always keep an eye on your horse when he is tied up. It takes only a few seconds for a horse to get into trouble and hurt himself!

QUICK-RELEASE KNOT

Always use a quick-release knot, which should come undone immediately with a strong tug on the free end. Here's how to tie one:

1 Thread the end of the lead rope through the loop made of safety string.

2 Form the loose end of the lead rope into a loop as shown.

3 Make another loop with the loose end and thread this under and through the first loop.

4 Leave the second loop hanging, then tighten the knot by pulling it and the rope attached to your horse at the same time.

5 To release the knot, pull on the loose end of the rope; it should come undone.

Better to horseproof the field. Walk around the pasture and run a safety check of the following.

FENCING

A pasture must have strong fencing without gaps or broken parts. Wooden post-and-rail fencing is traditional-looking and strong, but it is prone to needing repair and replacement due to weather and insect problems. Wood rots, splinters, and warps. Additionally, horses chew wood fencing.

There are better materials available today for every horse owner's set-up. Mesh or "no-climb" wire fencing has a springy texture that flexes to guard against injury, and is designed to keep intruders from scaling the fence. Synthetic fencing, such as polyvinyl chloride (PVC), high-tensile polymer rail, and coated wood, all are known for their strength, longevity, and low maintenance. Electric fencing teaches horses to respect fence lines and is appropriate for temporary and permanent use, but it must be maintained. A horse owner must keep the electric fence's lines taught and free of tall grasses, which may short out the fence. Additionally, this type of fencing is not completely horseproof, as a frightened horse can run right through the hot wire. Whichever fence you select, it should be at least 4 feet high; an athletic horse can jump over anything lower.

Never ever put your horse in a field with barbed-wire fencing. It was developed to withstand the tough hides of cattle, not the delicate skin of a horse. It is extremely dangerous and can cause serious injury.

GATES

A gate should be as tall as the surrounding fence, made of strong material, and locked securely with a horseproof latch. A clever horse will figure out how to open a gate and will do it over and over. You can buy horseproof latches at a tack store or a farm-and-feed store.

NATURAL HAZARDS

Walk around the field to make sure there are no holes. Fill in any holes you find with rocks and dirt. A hole can break a horse's leg. Put a barrier around a huge hole.

Look for fruit-bearing trees. Pick up ripened fruit before your horse gets it. Some horses get colic (a dangerous stomachache) after pigging out on ripening apples. Cherry tree leaves, red maple leaves, and oak tree acorns can also be dangerous. Check for poisonous plants, such as yew and hemlock, and remove them. Many ornamental flowers and bushes are toxic to horses too, so don't plant them in or near your field.

The American Society for the Prevention of Cruelty to Animals' website lists many plants that are toxic to horses. If you think your horse may have ingested a poisonous substance, contact your vet or the ASPCA's poison hotline (listed in the Resources chapter on page 92).

WATER

A field must have a constant supply of clean, fresh water from a tap. A horse drinks 5 to 20 gallons of water a day, or more if it's hot, if she gets a lot of exercise, or if she eats alfalfa hay regularly. Without enough water, your horse could get dehydrated and sick.

Water can be kept in a trough, a plastic barrel, or an old bathtub, provided it has no sharp edges or rust. You may have to fill it every day with a hose, or you can get a plumber to set up an automatic waterer with a valve.

Check the trough every day in the winter to make sure the water hasn't frozen, and break the ice, if necessary. You can also put a big rubber ball in the trough. If your horse doesn't take it out and play with it, the ball should float around and keep the water from freezing. There are also many brands of waterers that feature heaters so that you don't have to worry about your horse not drinking because the water is frozen or too cold.

SHELTER

Some type of shelter is necessary in a pasture. Ideally, there should be a run-in barn or shed. If not, the pasture should have some trees to offer cover from rain and give shade in the summer.

Your horse's pasture must have a fresh water supply.

SPACE

The pasture should have at least one acre of room per horse. If you put too many horses in a small field, they will eat all the grass and ruin the grazing. If you have two fields, rotate the horses between them so the grasses have time to grow again.

Routine Pasture Checks

If your horse is going to spend any time in a field, here are some jobs that you must be prepared to do on a regular basis.

EVERY DAY

Check twice a day to make sure your horse is comfortable and free from injuries; don't just wave at her from the other side of the fence.

Go in and take a closer look. Clean out her hooves with a hoof pick. If she wears shoes, make sure they're still on. If a shoe is missing, find it. If the shoe has nails sticking out, a horse could step on them and get a serious puncture wound.

Check the water supply and clean out the trough. Old leaves and rubbish can make the water taste bad, and a horse might not want to drink.

EVERY WEEK

Go into the pasture and shovel piles of manure onto a muck heap. This job is unglamorous, but it will keep your horse's grazing appetite healthy. Horses are fussy eaters and tend to avoid grass that has manure on it. Manure also attracts pesky flies and is a terrific home for worm eggs. You could also pay a local farmer to harrow the field with a tractor and spread the manure.

Check all the fences and make sure they're not broken. Pick up any rubbish that has blown into the pasture.

Picking up manure piles can cut down on flies.

A pen should be partially covered.

Paddocks

In some parts of the United States, especially the Southwest, many people house their horses in paddocks or corrals. A paddock for a single horse should be at least 12 feet by 24 feet in size, and partially covered so the horse has shelter from the elements. It should have a soft, fresh, thick bedding of shavings or sand, with new bedding added a couple times a month. If your horse lies down, she won't be comfortable on a hard dirt floor, nor will she stay clean. A pen must be cleaned and mucked out every day. It should also have a steady supply of water. If yours has an automatic waterer, check it every day to make sure it's working properly. Your horse's life depends on having fresh water throughout the day and evening hours, even when you are not around. Your attention to detail in the paddock will make all the difference for your horse's health and comfort.

Stables and Stalls

There are many different types of barns and stables, but most are sectioned off inside with box stalls for individual horses. A stall must be big enough for a horse to walk around and lie down. A 12-foot by 10-foot stall is suitable for a pony up to 14.2 hands high, but a horse needs an area 12 feet by 12 feet or more. The ceiling should be at least 10 feet from the ground so your horse won't bang her head if she rears.

The stall must have a large door, at least 4 feet wide, with plenty of space to pass through. For safety reasons, it should open outward. Most stall doors are divided so you can close the bottom and open the top, allowing your horse to look out and get some air. It's best to have two bolts on the door—one at the top and one at the bottom.

A barn or stable should be well ventilated, preferably with a window. Protect any window glass on the inside with strong wire mesh or bars. Keep the barn doors open. If the barn is constantly sealed tight, dust can cause breathing problems. A light is necessary, but it must be covered and out of your horse's reach. A stall should also have two sturdy metal rings bolted into the wall—one for a hay net and one to tie your horse to when you groom her.

BEDDING

Cover the stable floor with soft, comfortable bedding; standing on concrete or a dirt floor can cause leg sores and lameness. Additionally, a dirt-only floor is unsanitary, as there is nothing to soak up urine or manure. Deep bedding prevents drafts and keeps a horse warm if she lies down. To test if you have enough bedding, stick a pitchfork in it. You shouldn't be able to feel the ground. Try to provide at least a foot of bedding. Here are two common types of bedding you'll find at your local tack or feed store:

Wood Shavings: Many people use shavings in their stables because they are comfortable for horses to lie on and fairly easy to keep clean.

These are low in dust and are excellent bedding for horses with breathing problems or allergies. They come in big plastic or paper sacks and are more expensive than other types of bedding, but they are worth it if for horses with special needs.

Straw: Straw is the least expensive bedding. It comes in open bales tied with twine. You'll need several bales to fill a stall. Store straw in a dry place; it gets moldy when wet and can make a horse ill. Straw can also be dusty and make a horse cough. Spend the extra money for the best straw available. Keep an eye on your horse's weight if she has straw in her stable because many horses find it tasty and munch on it.

Lift out wet patches and droppings.

MUCKING OUT

You must clean, or muck out, a stall every day. This is when you remove the manure and wet patches and leave behind unsoiled bedding. Most people find it easiest to do one big muck-out a day.

If you do not clean a stall regularly, it will become dirty, smelly, and unhygienic, and your horse and her blankets will be impossible to keep clean. Wet bedding can give your horse thrush (a nasty hoof infection) and respiratory problems.

You need certain tools to muck out a stall. These can be purchased at most tack shops, farm equipment centers, and hardware stores for a reasonable price. Remember to keep them in a dry and safe place where a horse (or human) can't step on them and get hurt. Do not use these tools for any other purpose to prevent the spread of disease from feces and urine.

You need:

- a broom

- a pitchfork

- a rake

- a wheelbarrow or big muck bucket

Here's what to do every day to keep your horse's stall fresh and clean:

1 Turn out your horse into a pasture or arena. It will be much easier to clean her stall if she's out of your way. Then use the pitchfork to lift out wet bedding and droppings. Once the pitchfork is loaded, shake it gently so clean bedding falls off and stays in the stall. Toss the dirty bedding into the wheelbarrow or muck bucket.

A stall will stay fresher if you pick out any droppings as they appear. Take five minutes to lift out new piles at night, and you'll have a cleaner horse in the morning.

What may be good for one person's horse may not be appropriate for another, so keep special circumstances in mind as well. Find out what kind of hay people feed, too. This may vary from area to area.

Feeding Rules

Here are ten time-honored feeding rules that every responsible horse owner should follow:

1 **Feed little but often.** Horses constantly process food, so their often-delicate digestive systems work best when they eat small amounts of food throughout the day. This is why it's better to feed a horse several small meals a day instead of one or even two. Three meals are best, especially if your horse is stabled all the time.

In the wild, horses graze continuously, which keeps their digestive systems working smoothly. If your horse is fortunate, he spends some time each day out in a field and can eat grass. If he lives in a pen or stable, give him hay to snack on.

Never give your horse too much food. This can cause colic, a serious equine stomachache. Horses aren't like humans. They don't stop eating when they are full, and they can't throw up. If a horse overeats, the food can cause intestinal blockages that can kill him. This is why you must always lock the feed-room door.

2 **Always have fresh water available.** Your horse must have an unlimited supply of water in his field or stable. If he doesn't get enough, he could become dehydrated or lose his appetite. Offer your horse water before you feed him. If you give it to him after he eats, he may gulp it down and wash the food through his digestive system too quickly. Excess water also causes some types of grains to swell in a horse's stomach, which can cause colic.

3 **Feed your horse at regular times.** Horses are creatures of habit. They like knowing when they're going to be fed each day. It gives them a sense of security. Feeding late or inconsistently can worry a horse and make him sick. If you're going away, tell the person taking care of your horse what time to feed him.

4 **Make diet changes gradually.** Horses have sensitive stomachs, and sudden changes can cause colic, nausea or general stomach discomfort. Mix the old food with the new for a few days, and then gradually increase the portion of the new food. If you change his hay from alfalfa to grass, for example, feed a combination of the two for a few days, then gradually finish off the old hay and continue feeding the new.

Introduce pasture grass slowly, especially in the spring when it is richest. If your horse has been inside all winter, eating too much spring grass could give him laminitis (founder), a nasty disease that poisons a horse's blood and causes lameness. Feed him hay before you turn him out and only let him graze for about an hour or so at first. If he seems okay, gradually increase the time he spends in the field.

5 **Feed a lot of roughage (food with fiber).** Fiber comes from foods such as hay and grass. A horse's digestive system requires fiber to keep it working smoothly. If your horse is stabled all the time—or has bare pasture—feed him fiber each day in the form of hay or hay cubes.

6 **Feed top-quality, fresh food.** Give your horse the best-quality food you can afford. Remove grain from its sack and store it in a metal bin or plastic garbage can to stay fresh and free of hungry mice. Keep the lid securely fastened, so your horse can't get in either. If you horse overeats, it could a danger.

Store hay off the ground on wooden pallets, and keep it covered so it doesn't get wet and moldy. Damp or dusty food can make your horse sick. Keep buckets and mangers clean. Scrub them regularly to keep them bacteria-free.

7 **Feed succulents.** Add something succulent (juicy) to your horse's feed every day. Apples and carrots are tasty and add variety and moisture to his diet.

A horse can drink more than 13 gallons of water each day.

A horse needs fibrous foods such as hay.

8 **Give your horse salt.** Put a salt block in your horse's field or stable so he can lick it whenever he wants. Salt is an essential mineral; a horse loses it when he sweats during exercise or in hot weather. Some feeds have salt in them, but your horse may need more if he does a lot of work in warm weather. There are two common types of block you will find at the tack store: pure white salt and a reddish-brown salt, which has added minerals.

9 **Wait an hour after feeding before exercise.** Your horse needs about an hour to digest his food properly before you ride him. The blood supply to a horse's muscles increases during exercise, causing the blood supply to his digestive system to decrease. This can upset your horse's digestion. If you have to interrupt your horse's breakfast, lunch, or dinner to ride, keep the exercise short and nonstrenuous.

10 **Feed according to need.** Every horse is different, so it's best to learn your horse's individual feeding needs. Obviously, a small pony is going to eat less than a large horse, and a horse who gets a lot of work needs more food than one who doesn't exercise.

Here are some feeding guidelines:

◣ There are special feeds for different ages. Ask your trainer what he or she recommends.

◣ A horse in a pen or stable has different dietary needs from a horse in a field.

◣ Too much feed can make a nervous horse behave badly. Keep an eye on behavior to gauge feed levels.

◣ Feed according to size. Buy a special measuring tape at the tack shop and use it to estimate your horse's weight. Your equine vet should have some recommendations for feeding according to weight and size.

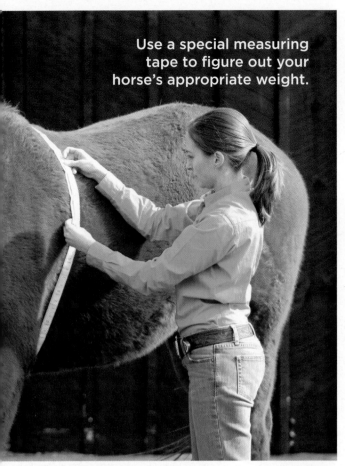

Use a special measuring tape to figure out your horse's appropriate weight.

Hay should smell fresh and clean.

Hay cubes are a source of roughage.

Sweet feed contains vitamins and nutrients that a horse needs.

▸ Feed according to type. A fuzzy mixed-breed has different dietary needs from a thin-skinned, purebred Arabian. You can always check with a local breeder for ideas on dietary needs associated with different breeds.

▸ Horses need more food in the winter; it takes a lot of energy to keep warm.

▸ The harder your horse works, the more feed he needs.

Food to Feed a Horse

There are two groups of horse feeds that you need to know about: roughage and concentrates. Your horse needs both in his diet to keep him healthy.

ROUGHAGE

Roughage is grass, hay, and hay cubes or pellets. A horse needs a lot of roughage to keep his digestive system working properly. Grass is the most natural type of food for horses. Different types of grass grow in different climates, and the quality of grass can vary from field to field.

Most horses get the bulk of their roughage from hay, which is grass that has been cut and dried, usually in the summer when it's most nutritious. Hay is usually stored in bales. If a horse doesn't get much work, he may thrive on a diet of hay only—provided that the hay is nutritious. Buy hay at a feed store or from a reputable local farmer.

The type and quality varies from area to area, so you may have to go through some trial and error before you find the ideal hay for your horse. Ask fellow horse people where they purchase high-quality hay. The most commonly found types of hay are:

Grass Hay: This is a low-energy, filling, and fairly inexpensive hay; it can be made from a variety of grasses.

Alfalfa Hay: Energy-giving, it is very nutritious, but can be too rich for some horses and is expensive.

Oat Hay: Oat hay is low-energy, filling, and usually inexpensive.

Timothy Hay: This variety of hay is low-energy, moderately nutritious grass hay.

Bermuda Hay: This grass hay is similar to Timothy in nutritional value.

Only buy hay that is greenish-yellow and smells sweet. Give it a good sniff before you feed it to your horse. Hay that is dusty, yellow, or moldy can make a horse ill and creates barn dust that is unhealthy for humans as well.

Some folks like to put their hay in a net and soak it in clean water for a few hours. Soaking hay removes some of the dust that can irritate a horse's lungs, and the hay can be eaten wet.

There is some debate over feeding horses on the ground versus feeding from a manger. A manger makes the horse eat with his head up, which is an unnatural position for his posture and digestive track. Feeding from the ground allows the horse to eat with his head in a more natural and comfortable position. However, hay gets wasted, and some horses ingest dirt from the ground along with their meal. A good compromise is feeding on a stall mat located on the ground.

Hay can be ground up, dried, and compressed into cubes or pellets. If you can't get good hay in your area, cubes are an excellent substitute because they're as nutritious as loose hay. Fussy horses may find them awkward to eat, but, in some facilities, hay cubes are the only feed given to the horses.

CONCENTRATES

Concentrates are foods that are high in nutritional value and fed in small amounts. They can be grains, mixed feeds, or pellets.

Use concentrates when your horse's nutritional needs are not being met by eating hay or grass. For example, if you're working your horse hard, he may not be getting enough energy from hay alone. If you want him to gain weight, you may have to feed him concentrates. A pregnant mare or a mare with a foal usually needs to eat concentrates to stay healthy. If your horse is retired or doesn't get much work, he probably doesn't need concentrates. If he's too energetic or nervous, decrease or eliminate his concentrates altogether. You'll come across some different kinds of concentrates:

Grains: Oats, corn, barley, and bran are the most common concentrates. Oats are high in energy; corn is full of protein; barley is good for adding weight; and bran acts as a laxative.

Experienced horse people sometimes mix grains to make their own hard feeds, but you have to be knowledgeable about equine nutrition and different grains' qualities before you attempt this. If you want to mix grains, consult someone who has some experience doing so.

Complete Feeds and Pellets: Complete feeds are usually a mixture of grains such as barley, oats, and corn. They also contain all of the vitamins and minerals a horse needs. They are developed by equine nutritionists and are easy to use because manufacturers specify on their products the amounts to feed your horse. The amounts usually are specified in pounds, so get a scale from a feed supply store or horse supply catalog and a big can or scoop to use to measure your feed accurately.

If you're a new horse owner, or simply want an uncomplicated life, feed your horse a complete feed or pellets. Combined with hay or grass, complete feeds or pellets should give your horse a well-rounded diet.

There are plenty of complete feeds and pellets to choose from at feed stores, and feed companies make different feeds to suit different types of horses. There are special feeds for pregnant mares, mares in foal, young horses, performance horses, and senior citizens. The most popular complete feeds seem to be "sweet feeds," mixtures that contain different types of grain moistened with molasses to make them extra tasty.

Pellets are a mixture of crushed grains, vitamins, and minerals. They can be bland and dry, though, and some horses find them boring to eat. Throw a few carrots and apples in with them to spice up your horse's mealtimes.

Cut carrots into finger-size segments and apples into quarters.

Vitamins and Supplements

If your horse eats a complete multigrain feed, he may be getting all the vitamins and minerals he needs. The information on the sack should state if the feed satisfies a horse's daily nutritional requirements.

But if your horse eats only hay or hay cubes, he may need a daily vitamin or mineral supplement, which you can find at a tack and feed store. They come in powder or pellet form, and you add them to your horse's meals each day. Some supplements include biotin, a vitamin that strengthens hooves. Others contain wheat germ or soybean oil and other essential fatty acids to make your horse's coat shiny.

A less-expensive way to bring out the shine in your horse's coat is to add a dollop of corn oil (about a quarter cup each day) to each of your horse's feeds. Corn oil contains fat, so it can also help a thin horse gain weight.

Electrolytes are supplements generally given to competition horses. They combine minerals that horses need to stay healthy, such as chloride, sodium, and potassium.

If your horse has access to a salt block and a nutritious diet, it's unlikely that he will need electrolytes—especially if he doesn't work very hard. If he does a lot of work—for instance, he's a three-day eventer or an endurance horse—he may need these minerals replenished after strenuous exercise. Horses who live in hot climates and sweat a lot may also need them. Consult your equine veterinarian before you make a decision about electrolytes for your horse.

Electrolytes usually come in powder form and are mixed into a horse's water. Do not use electrolytes unless your vet says that your horse needs them.

It's best to feed your horse using a bucket, but you should hold your hand flat when giving treats, if you feed by hand.

Treats

Horses love carrots and apples, which are good for them. You can buy special horse treats that look like cookies, but don't give your horse candy or sugar cubes. They're bad for his teeth.

Cut apples into quarters and carrots into finger-size segments to make them easy for your horse to chew. Smaller pieces can get stuck in his throat and cause him to choke.

Giving treats by hand is a bad idea because your horse will come to expect them and may bite or bother you for them. Be sensible and feed treats in a bucket. If you must feed a treat by hand, when you are catching your horse, for example, hold your hand flat and put the treat on it. Never hold the treat with your fingers because your horse may nibble them instead of the tidbit.

A Horse's Health

your horse should have her own equine veterinarian, someone you trust who knows your horse inside and out. Choose a local vet who can get to your horse quickly in an emergency.

If you keep your horse at a boarding facility, put a emergency contact card on her stall door with the names and numbers of both you and your vet. A passerby who notices your horse is ill can call you both. But don't count on others to make sure your horse is healthy, especially at a big, busy barn. It's your responsibility. Check your horse every day to make sure she is okay. This means looking at her from head to hoof.

These signs tell you your horse feels great:

- She's alert and interested in what's going on around her.

- Her ears move around, and she listens for interesting sounds.

- She eats all of her food.

- She has a shiny coat.

- Her legs and hooves are cool to the touch.

- She puts weight on all four feet.

- Her droppings are firm and ball-shaped.

Here are signs that tell you to call the vet:

- Your horse looks depressed and hangs her head low.

- She's listless and doesn't move around.

- She doesn't eat or finish her food.

- She doesn't drink water.

- She limps and keeps her weight off a particular leg.

- She coughs or has a runny nose or eyes.

- She has runny droppings.

- Her coat is dull and has bare patches.

- She nips at her stomach or rolls violently (signs of colic).

Taking Your Horse's Temperature

If you suspect your horse is sick, take her temperature. It's not difficult. Keep a veterinary thermometer in your tack box. It should have a long safety string with a clip on the end. If it doesn't, tie on a long ribbon or piece of string with a clothespin on the end of it. Clip the ribbon or string to your horse's tail so the thermometer can't disappear inside her or fall on the ground.

Shake the thermometer so it reads below 97° F. To insert the device easily, dip it in petroleum jelly.

A horse's temperature should be between 100° F and 101° F.

Lift your horse's tail and gently slide the thermometer into her rectum, leaving about half of it outside. Keep it in place for two minutes, then take it out, wipe it clean, and read it. The temperature of a healthy horse should be between 100° F and 101° F. If it is any higher or lower and the horse has symptoms of distress, call the vet.

Health Problems

CHOKING

Choking is caused by something getting stuck in your horse's esophagus. It can happen when you feed her large, lumpy foods such as hay cubes, which she may not chew properly. If a horse is choking, she will stop eating and may panic. She will drool, and food may come out of her nose.

Touch her neck to see if you can feel a lumpy obstruction. If you can, call the vet immediately, and encourage the horse to drink some water, which may push the food down her throat.

Prevent choking by giving your horse an unlimited supply of water, cutting carrots and apples into easy-to-chew sizes, and placing bricks or big rocks in your horse's manger to prevent her from gulping food.

COLIC

Colic is an equine stomachache caused by many things, including:

- a change in the weather
- a change of feed
- damage to her stomach or intestines caused by worms
- overeating
- swallowing dirt or sand along with feed
- stress

A horse with colic may pace around her stall. She may nip or kick at her stomach, or lie down and roll. Sometimes, her only symptoms will be lethargy and depression. When you call the vet, describe the behavior, and the vet will tell you what to do until he or she arrives.

You may have to walk the horse. Gentle exercise can help the obstruction to move through her digestive system. It's a good sign if she passes wind or manure because she will soon feel better. If your horse seems depressed, leave her alone. Don't force her to walk; if she's cold, blanket her.

Sometimes the colic is only gas-related, and can be relieved with drugs. But sometimes a horse has a blockage in the intestine that cannot move on its own. If your horse is rolling violently, then the colic is serious. Get her up on her feet right away. Rolling can twist her intestines and kill her. When the vet arrives, he or she may give your horse a tranquilizer if she's upset or moving around too much. Then the vet may lubricate the horse's intestines with mineral oil. This involves running a flexible hose down her nose and pumping mineral oil into her stomach. The oil helps to ease dangerous food blockages through a horse's digestive system, and she should recover in a couple of hours.

If this doesn't work, the horse will require surgery in order to stay alive. This is why you need to be aware of how your horse feels at all times; the sooner you see something amiss, the better your horse's chances of pulling through.

HEAVES

Heaves, sometimes called "Chronic Obstructive Pulmonary Diseases" (or COPD), is a lung condition that makes it hard for a horse to breathe properly. Sometimes when a horse eats moldy, dusty hay or continually lives in dusty surroundings, she develops an allergic reaction. Her lungs become weak and she must use her abdominal muscles to push the air out of her lungs. An affected horse heaves when she breathes, and coughs a lot. It used to be that a horse with heaves was considered to have

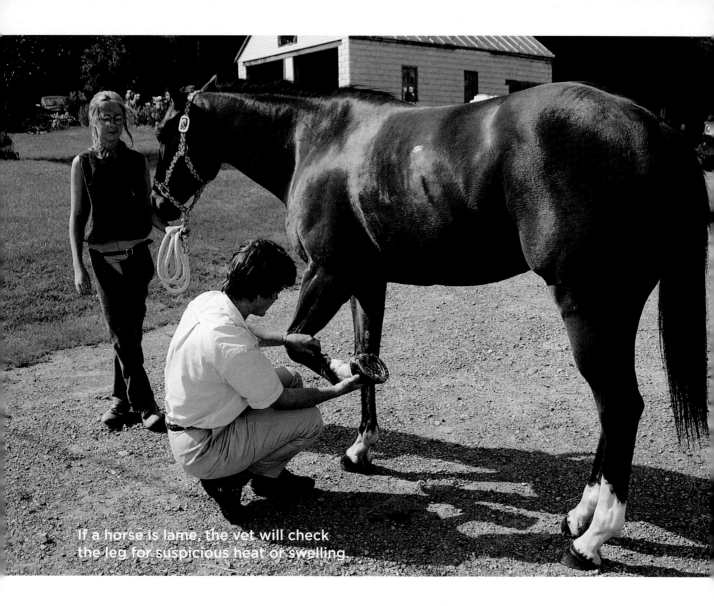

If a horse is lame, the vet will check the leg for suspicious heat or swelling.

"broken wind" and could not be cured, thus ending any serious riding career. But today, horses can recover from heaves if they are turned out to pasture or moved into a well-ventilated stall; fed cubed or pelleted roughage with dampened grain; and kept on dust and mold-free bedding such as shredded paper or high-quality wood shavings.

LAMENESS

Signs of lameness are limping and trying to take weight off one leg. The horse may also bob her head up and down when she moves or be extra bumpy when you ride her. Before you call the vet, check her legs for the following:

- a cut that needs to be cleaned and medicated

- a rock or other debris, such as a nail, stuck in the hoof. Use a hoof pick to get rid of

debris, then soak the hoof in ¾ cup of Epsom salts mixed in a bucket of warm water for 15 minutes. This soothes minor soreness.

- stone bruises. These are common and happen when your horse steps on a rock or another hard object and bruises her sole or heel. Soak the area in ¾ cup of Epsom salts mixed in a bucket of warm water for 15 minutes several times over a couple of days, and put some "bute" (a nonsteroidal anti-inflammatory, similar to ibuprofen) in her feed. If the soreness doesn't go away after a few days, call the vet.

- loose nails from her shoes or nails sticking into the sensitive hoof wall. An outgrown shoe could be pinching her feet. In this case, call the farrier to remove the shoe, or pull it off yourself if you know how.

- Lumps that could be splints. Splints are bony growths on the lower legs, usually caused by working a young horse too hard. When splints are new, they can be painful, so rest your horse for a while. If the lameness goes away, it's unlikely the splint will cause more damage, but it will look unsightly. If the lameness continues, the splint may need veterinary attention.

- a pulled muscle, tendon or ligament. The vet will have to examine the horse to find out what is causing the lameness. Always rest a lame horse, and if the condition persists, put her in a stall that restricts her movement and call the vet.

LAMINITIS (FOUNDER)

Laminitis is a serious metabolic condition that can make a horse lame. It is usually caused by overeating, such as when a horse eats too much rich grass or breaks into the feed room and overeats. Laminitis releases toxins into the bloodstream that travel down to the hooves and damage the circulation of the feet. It affects either the front feet or all four. The laminae, which is the sensitive tissue that attaches the hoof wall to the horse's coffin bone, becomes inflamed, and the horse suffers great pain. Her hooves feel hot, rings may appear around her hoof wall, and her toes may curl up. She may lean backward to take her weight off her hooves.

If you think your horse has laminitis, remove her feed and call the vet. She may tell you to hose the hooves until she arrives. Then she may put a horse with laminitis in a special "diet" paddock with little grass, or she may cut down her feed and prescribe medicine. Sadly, once a horse suffers a laminitis attack, you have to be careful about her diet because it can recur.

MUD FEVER (CRACKED HEELS)

If your horse lives in a muddy field or her stable gets wet, her heels or pasterns can get chapped and sore and can start splitting. If this happens, keep her footing as dry as possible, and keep her pastern and heels clean. Trim stray hairs away from the infected area and apply an antibacterial ointment.

To prevent mud fever, keep your horse's heels dry. Don't hose off her legs every day, especially in the winter. If her legs get muddy, wait for them to dry, then brush them off. It may help to apply petroleum jelly to her heels in wet weather.

NAVICULAR DISEASE

If your horse is constantly lame, she may have navicular disease—a painful condition that affects the navicular bone inside the hoof and the attached tendon. Both become inflamed, causing soreness in the hoof. A horse with navicular takes short, stiff steps. The condition can be caused by:

- bad shoeing

- lack of regular hoof care

- poor hoof and leg conformation

- too much work on hard footing

If your horse is diagnosed with navicular disease, your farrier may put special shoes on her to make her more comfortable, and she may require regular medicine. Don't give up on a horse with navicular disease because she may be able to continue to do her job as long as her condition is maintained.

RINGWORM

Ringworm is a nasty fungus that causes your horse's hair to fall out in the shape of a circle. It is highly contagious to you and other animals, so isolate her and wash your hands and tools in a disinfectant solution after touching her. Don't use her brushes and blankets on any other horses. Your vet should give you an antibacterial cream and a medicated wash to use on the infected area.

THRUSH

Thrush is a bacterial disease that affects the frog area—the V-shaped cleft in the hoof. Horses who stand in wet or dirty footing are likely to get thrush. It's easy to spot because the infected hoof has a bad odor, and the frog is crumbly and covered in a gooey, black substance.

If your horse gets thrush, keep her hooves completely dry. Your vet or farrier may tell you to soak the hoof in an antibacterial solution or apply medicine to the infected area.

The easiest way to avoid thrush is to pick out your horse's hooves every day and keep her stable or pen clean and dry.

Regular Veterinary Checkups

The best way to maintain a healthy horse is to have regular vet checkups. Once or twice a year is usually enough. The vet listens to your horse's heart and takes her temperature. She checks her legs to make sure they are free of injuries.

One of the most important things the vet should do regularly is float, or rasp, your horse's teeth. She uses a big metal file to level out any sharp edges on your horse's teeth so she can eat properly. Once a year is usually enough; young and old horses may need more frequent floatings.

VACCINATIONS AND TESTS

When your vet comes for a checkup, she also vaccinates your horse. Vaccinations vary from area to area, depending on which viruses exist in your state. If you plan to show your horse, she'll need certain shots, and show organizers often ask you to bring your veterinary records so they can check that she has had her shots. Here are some shots or tests the vet may give your horse:

Tetanus (lockjaw): This infection of the nervous system can happen if a horse steps on a rusty nail or gets a deep cut. The horse's muscles stiffen so badly that she can barely move. Most tetanus cases are fatal. A shot is given once a year.

Influenza (flu): The flu is a contagious, airborne virus. When one horse has the flu, others at the facility will likely get it too. A horse with the flu has a runny nose and may cough. Two or three shots a year is normal to prevent it.

Encephalomyelitis (sleeping sickness): This deadly virus is carried by mosquitoes. A horse contracts a fever and then becomes paralyzed. A yearly vaccination is usually recommended.

Rabies: If there have been cases of animals with rabies in your area, your vet may vaccinate your horse against the disease. Luckily, horses rarely get rabies.

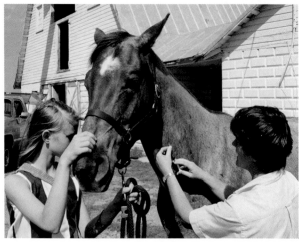

A horse needs her teeth floated (top) at least once a year. However, equine vaccinations vary from area to area (bottom).

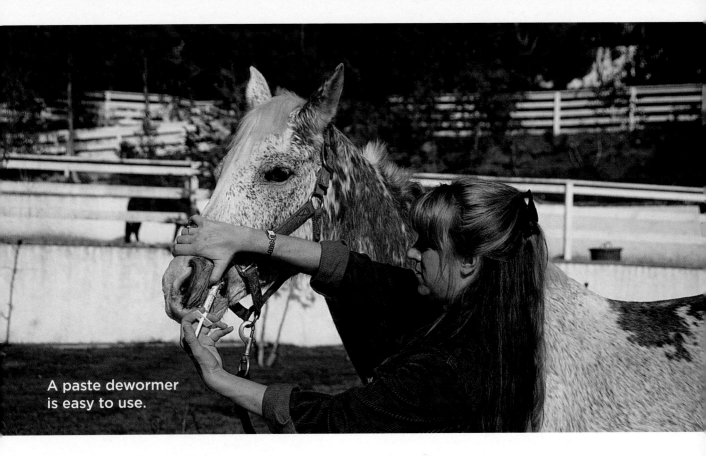

A paste dewormer is easy to use.

Equine Infectious Anemia (swamp fever): This is another deadly virus that lives in a horse's blood and is passed from horse to horse by biting insects, such as mosquitoes. Unfortunately, there is no vaccination at this time for this disease, but there is a test called a Coggins test that shows if your horse has been exposed to the virus. Many show organizers will ask to see your Coggins test results. If your horse is a carrier of the virus, she has to be put down.

WORMING

Horses are constantly exposed to internal parasites (worms), so they must be dewormed on a regular basis. Worms can damage a horse's blood vessels, intestines, lungs, and heart. A horse with a worm infestation is thin and sickly because most of the parasites live in the digestive tract and make it difficult for the horse to process food effectively. Wormy horses often suffer colic attacks.

Generally, parasites lay eggs in a horse's stomach. The eggs then travel through the digestive system and come out in the manure. They hatch into tiny larvae that crawl onto blades of grass. A horse eats the grass, and the cycle starts again.

Some worms can make your horse ill:

- Large strongyles (bloodworms) and small strongyles damage a horse's blood vessels, digestive system, and other internal organs. They sometimes cause colic, which can kill a horse.

- Ascarids live in a horse's small intestine and are often found in foals and young horses.

- Pinworms irritate a horse's rectum; an afflicted horse may rub her tail and rear end a lot.

- Bot flies lay eggs on a horse's skin, usually around her legs, shoulders, and chin. They look like little yellow dots. When the eggs hatch, the larvae find their way to the horse's mouth and are swallowed. Some mature into bots, which stick to the stomach wall and cause ulcers. Others are expelled with manure and hatch into bot flies. If you see bot eggs on your horse, scrape them off carefully with a razor blade.

Tapeworms, hairworms, lungworms, intestinal threadworms, and stomach worms round out some of the major types of internal parasites that plague horses.

Deworm your horse on a regular schedule, usually every eight to twelve weeks. You can buy dewormer at a tack shop, from a catalog, or from your vet. There are different dewormers for different parasites, so ask your vet which one to use. Veterinarians usually recommend that you rotate dewormers because some parasites can develop immunities to certain wormers if they are used repeatedly.

Dewormers come in pelleted form, which is added to feed, or a paste. The pastes come in an oral syringe (no needle). The numbers on the side of the syringe tell you how much to give your horse, depending on her weight. (If you don't know how much your horse weighs, buy a special measuring tape to determine her approximate weight.) Set the plunger at your horse's weight. Cradling her muzzle with your arm underneath her jaw, slide the syringe into the corner of her mouth.

Then press the plunger so that the paste squirts onto the back of her tongue. Hold her head up for a minute after you remove the syringe so you can be sure she swallows the paste.

Here are some other ways to prevent worms:

Remove manure piles from your horse's field on a regular basis.

Keep food away from manure.

Don't crowd too many horses into a tiny field or pen.

Rest a pasture (take the horses out) for a couple of months to break the worm's life cycle.

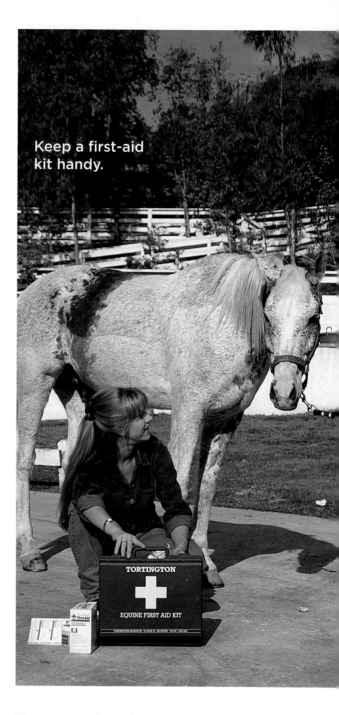

Keep a first-aid kit handy.

First Aid

Always be prepared for an emergency. Keep a first-aid kit handy and post your vet's phone number where it can be easily seen. Replace items as you use them. Here is what should be in your first-aid kit:

absorbent sheets of cotton and cotton balls

adhesive tape

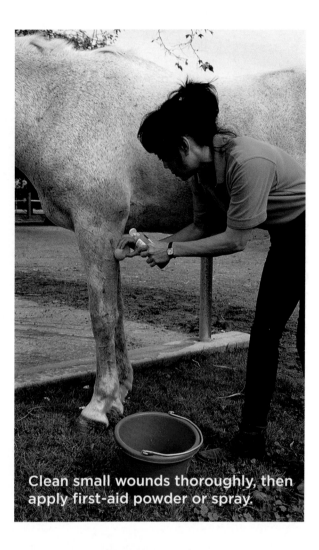

Clean small wounds thoroughly, then apply first-aid powder or spray.

- clean sponges (a couple)

- disinfectant or antiseptic solution (povidone iodine) for cleaning cuts

- epsom salts

- gauze roll and gauze squares

- saline solution and large syringe to irrigate wounds

- scissors

- several rolls of self-adhesive stretch bandage

Use a bandage to apply pressure to a bleeding wound.

you've used a curry comb and a dandy brush. It is a great all-purpose brush to bring out the coat's shine. Because it's relatively soft, the body brush can be used on a horse's head and other sensitive places, such as his stomach.

Finishing Brush: These are usually the softest brushes in your kit, and they are used to whisk the fine dust off a groomed coat.

Mane Comb: This small metal or plastic comb can untangle a horse's mane and tail. There are also smaller combs for pulling a horse's mane. These flat-backed brushes detangle without pulling out tail hairs. An inexpensive human hairbrush works well on the mane and tail, too.

Stable Cloth: The soft cloth removes stains or polishes a horse's coat. Make a few by cutting an old towel into small squares.

Sponges: Your grooming kit should have several big, soft sponges. Use one for cleaning your horse's eyes and nose, and another for under his tail (the dock area). Using only one sponge for both areas spreads bacteria and infections. Use different colored sponges so you can tell them apart.

Bath Mitt: Whether pebble-palmed, honeycombed or open weave, these brushes distribute shampoo on the horse's coat, but rinse clean quickly, unlike a sponge, which holds shampoo (and often dirt and hair) in.

Sweat Scraper: A plastic or metal tool to remove excess water from your horse after a bath so he dries more quickly.

Water Brush: A brush with long, firm bristles to dampen the mane or tail, it is also used to clean mud from hooves.

Your grooming kit needs a good cleaning itself at least once a month. Use shampoo or detergent to wash your brushes and let them dry.

Get Grooming!

Tie your horse somewhere safe, away from other horses, using a quick-release knot (see page 19).

1 Start your grooming session by picking out your horse's hooves with the hoof pick.

2 Next, rub the curry comb in a circular motion on your horse's neck. Dirt will rise to the coat's surface. Work your way back to the horse's hindquarters, but don't use a curry comb on sensitive areas such as the head or lower legs.

3 Use the dandy brush in short, firm strokes to sweep away the dirt you have turned up with the curry comb. Brush in the direction the hair grows. Start at the top of your horse's neck and work back to his hindquarters so you don't brush dirt onto parts you've already cleaned.

4 Next, use the soft body brush. It removes fine dirt and adds shine. Also use the body brush on your horse's head and lower legs. To clean the dandy brush and the body brush, scrape them on a metal curry comb, and the dirt should fly off.

5 Your finishing brush can be used to take any dust off your horse's shiny coat. You can skip this step if you are doing a general-purpose grooming.

6 Dampen the eye/nose sponge with clean water, and gently wipe your horse's eyes and nose. Wet the other sponge and clean the dock area.

7 Finally, use your fingers to untangle the mane and tail. Then brush them with the hairbrush or a dandy brush. If you use a metal mane comb, be gentle because it can break the hair and cause equine frizzies. When you work on your horse's tail, stand to one side, not right behind the horse. If he spooks, you don't want to get stepped on or kicked.

8 If your horse has stains, dampen a stable cloth and remove them. Use a dry cloth to buff him, making his coat sleek and shiny.

Use a rubber curry comb in circles.

You can buy equine stain remover at tack shops; it's particularly handy if you have a gray horse (gray horse coats stain more easily).

PULLING THE MANE

If you want your horse's mane to look neat and tidy, you consider pulling or thinning it. For some breeds, such as Arabians, Morgans, and Andalusians, however, it's traditional to leave the mane (and tail) long and flowing. If you plan to show your horse in breed classes, learn the requirements before you start pulling.

Use a small metal comb designed for pulling. Never use scissors on the mane because it will grow back unevenly and look ragged. Only pull a horse's mane after he has exercised—when he's warm and the pores of his skin are open. The hair pulls out more easily. Pull only for a few minutes at a time. Some horses dislike having their manes pulled because it stings, so complete your pulling over several sessions to avoid causing pain to the horse's tender skin. Here's how you do it:

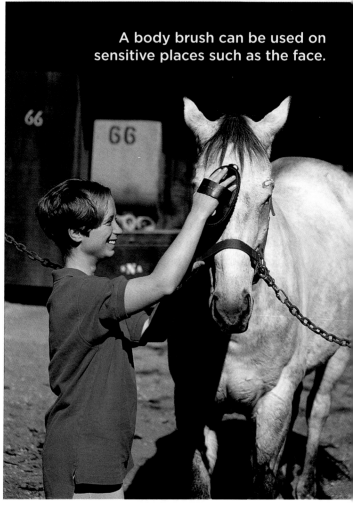

A body brush can be used on sensitive places such as the face.

1 Start at the top of the neck. Comb out a very small section of hair. Then tease back the shorter hairs, so that you are only holding the longest 10 or 12 strands.

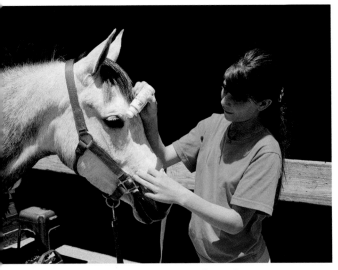

Roll-on fly sprays are handy to use around the ears and eyes.

Pick out your horse's hooves every day, and use the hoof pick from heel to toe.

Use fly barriers, including masks, fly sheets, ear bonnets, and fly socks.

Hoof Care

With a hoof pick, clean your horse's hooves every day—before and after you ride. Hooves get packed with mud or stones and make your horse lame. Here's how to use a hoof pick:

1 Start with the left foreleg and face your horse's tail. Run your hand down his leg so he knows you are going to pick up his hoof.

2 He should pick up his hoof when you touch the pastern just above the hoof. If he refuses to cooperate, you can pinch the area just above his fetlock, pinch the scaly chestnut on the inside of his leg, or you can lean against him with your shoulder until he takes the weight off the foot you want to pick up.

3 Hold the hoof in your left hand and the hoof pick in your right. Use the pointed end of the pick to remove debris. Always work from the heel (the back of the hoof) to the toe (the front). Take special care to clean out the dirt in the V-shaped groove around the frog. When you finish, put his foot down gently on the ground.

4 Pick out the rear hoof in the same way, looking backward again. Stand next to the horse, not behind him.

5 Pick out the hooves on the other side, starting with the foreleg. You can wash the outside of the hoof with a brush and water.

HOOF OIL AND DRESSINGS
If you live in a dry climate, hooves may dry out and crack. For this condition, some suggest regularly applying hoof oil or dressing to the bottom of the hoof and the hoof wall. Hoof oil or dressing

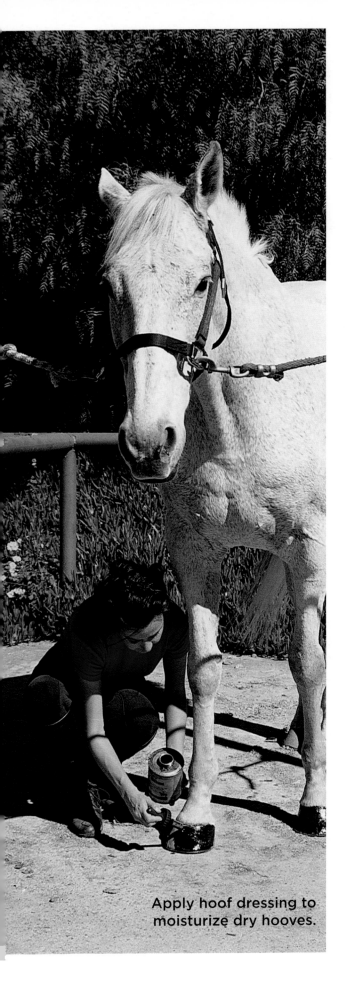

Apply hoof dressing to moisturize dry hooves.

moisturizes hooves. But abundant use can also make hooves too soft. Many farriers recommend that you only put oil at the coronary band of the hoof, where there is new growth.

If your horse's hooves seem weak or are chipping, your farrier or vet may advise you to add a special hoof supplement to his diet. You can buy this at a tack shop or feed store. Some supplements contain biotin, a B-complex vitamin that helps to strengthen hooves.

The Farrier

The farrier will trim your horse's hooves and put shoes on him if needed. A horse's hooves are like human nails. They grow about a quarter of an inch a month, so they need to be trimmed and filed (rasped) into shape every five to six weeks. If your horse's hooves get too long, they affect his gaits and make it difficult for him to move properly. He could also become sore and lame.

Most riding horses wear shoes made of iron, steel, or aluminum to protect their feet. Horses ridden on rocky trails, roads, or hard ground need shoes to prevent their hooves from wearing down.

If your horse has hoof problems, a farrier may make specially designed shoes to help the hooves grow normally. Special shoes are also used on horses with gait or movement problems caused by conformation defects or disease.

If your horse is not ridden on hard surfaces or spends all his time in a pasture, he may not need shoes, but he still needs his hooves trimmed. Trimming is less expensive than shoeing.

Ask your instructor or a horse-owning friend to recommend an experienced farrier. If he has shod a horse in your barn, check out his work before you make an appointment. You may not understand the subtleties of shoeing, but you will be able to determine whether he does the work himself, or whether an apprentice helps. You will also see his manner around horses.

Tack
and Gear

*t*he bridle, saddle, and other equipment you use on your horse are called "tack." You can buy tack at a tack shop or order it from a catalog.

You can also buy used tack at an auction, from a consignment shop, or even from a private owner on the Internet, but be observant when purchasing used equipment. The tack could have loose stitching, rotten leather, or a broken saddle tree. Study it carefully and ask questions about its care before you pay for it.

English and western riding each has its own kind of tack, so buy tack for your style of riding. If you want to jump, a bulky western saddle is not for you. If you want to trail ride for hours, a flat jumping saddle won't be very comfortable. Visit a tack shop or look at a catalog with your instructor or a horsey friend, and ask them to advise you on what's best for your particular needs. Also, check out the gear that other people at your barn are using. Here is what you need to start.

The Halter

A halter is a head collar made of leather or strong nylon. Like a dog's collar, it gives you control over your horse when you're not riding her. A halter has no bit, so you can tie her while she's wearing it. Most halters have a metal ring underneath the horse's jaw, where you clip a lead rope (your horse's leash). Lead ropes are made of cotton or nylon.

If your horse is frisky or disobedient when you lead her, fasten a chain to the lead rope and run it over her nose. This gives you extra control, but never tie your horse using a chain because she could injure her face if she pulls back.

The Bridle

A bridle buckles over your horse's head and is used to guide and cue your horse. They can be made of leather or a synthetic material and come in several sizes: pony, cob (a large pony or small horse), and

This horse is wearing an English bridle with a simple cavesson noseband.

horse. Bridles consist of a headstall, a bit, and a set of reins. Bridles have buckles and hooks to help you adjust them to fit your horse perfectly.

ENGLISH BRIDLES

Almost all English or hunt-seat bridles look the same. They consist of:

- a crown (or head) piece with a throatlatch attached to it

- two cheekpieces, which attach to the bit

- a noseband

- a browband

- reins, which attach to the bit

- a bit, which goes in the horse's mouth

WESTERN BRIDLES

Western headstalls are often flashier than their English counterparts. They may be decorated with fancy stitching, silver buckles, silver beads (called "ferrules"), and silver or metal coin-size decorations (called "conchas"). They come in two main styles: a browband style, similar to English bridles, and a slip-ear style, which has a loop in the crown piece where the ear pokes through.

Like English-style bridles, most western headstalls have a bit that is fastened to cheekpieces and reins. But most western headstalls do not have a noseband.

Reins

Reins attach to the bit that goes in your horse's mouth. They are one or two straps that you hold in your hands. The open or split rein is a commonly used western rein. It is made of two separate straps, ⅜ to 1 inch wide and about 6 to 8 feet long, with decorative braiding on the ends.

The two straps cross over the withers. Pulling on a rein puts pressure on the bit, which then puts pressure on your horse's mouth. This pressure tells your horse to slow down, stop, or turn.

Bits

Bits are made of stainless steel, rubber, or nylon, and they come in different sizes. If a bit is too small, it pinches and hurts your horse's mouth. If it's too big, it won't work properly.

There are hundreds of bits to choose from. Some bits are mild; others are strong and can hurt a horse's mouth—especially if a rider has rough hands. If you're just starting out or have a young horse, it's best to use a mild bit, such as a snaffle or a low port curb bit. If your horse is extra strong, you may need to try other bits until you find one that enables you to control your horse.

THE SNAFFLE

Snaffle bits are used by both western and English riders. They have two rings, which attach to the bridle, and a mouthpiece, which is

This western bridle is suitable for showing.

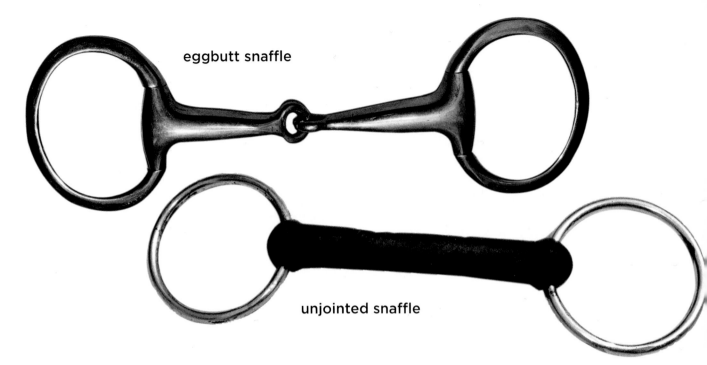

eggbutt snaffle

unjointed snaffle

hinged to the rings. The mouthpiece may be unjointed (one piece) or jointed (two pieces joined in the middle). The thinner the mouthpiece, the more severe the bit. If a snaffle has a thick mouthpiece, it is probably quite mild. However, if your horse has a small mouth, a thick bit is actually uncomfortable, so find one that is right for your horse's anatomy.

Here are a few types of snaffles you could try on your horse:

D-Ring: A D-ring snaffle is a single-jointed bit with a rubber or metal mouthpiece. The fixed D-shaped rings at each end prevent the bit from being pulled through the horse's mouth. This is a great bit for a quiet or young horse, and it is the most popular style bit for show hunters.

Full Cheek: This bit has 4- to 5-inch-long cheekpieces that put pressure on the sides of the horse's mouth and cheek, giving the rider more steering power. If your horse is hard to turn, this is the bit for her.

Eggbutt: The rings on the side of the eggbutt bit are welded to the mouthpiece. This is a mild bit, often seen at shows on dressage horses.

Unjointed: An unjointed snaffle is often made of rubber and is very mild. It is often used on young horses. It is sometimes called a "dog-bone bit."

Loose Ring (sometimes called an "O-ring" by western riders): The rings on the sides of this mild bit are not fixed to the mouthpiece. This lets the mouthpiece move around

in a horse's mouth. Many horses play with their mouthpieces, which produces saliva that keeps their mouths soft and responsive to the bit. A loose ring snaffle is often used on youngsters and dressage horses.

Twisted: This severe snaffle has a twisted mouthpiece, and it feels rough against the horse's mouth when you pull on the reins. When she slows down, relieve the pressure in her mouth by softening your hold on the reins. This bit is often used on strong horses who pull a lot.

If you can't stop or control your horse effectively in a snaffle, try another type of bit.

Curb Bits

Many English and western riders use bits from the curb family. A curb bit encourages a horse to lower her head, which makes the bit work more effectively. Curb bits are usually shaped like a capital H. They have long cheekpieces and often have unjointed mouthpieces.

Curb bits work by leverage. When you apply your hand's pressure to a rein (attached to a ring on the bottom of the bit), the top of the bit moves forward pulling the bridle down so it presses on your horse's poll. She then lowers her head.

Curb bits have a small chain that goes under the horse's jaw. When you pull on the reins, the chain presses on the horse's jaw and encourages her to flex more. Here are some popular curb bits:

The Basic Curb Bit: Used by most western riders, this bit is made of metal and is usually unjointed. Most western curbs have a raised port—a bump in the middle of the mouthpiece. The port puts extra pressure on a horse's tongue and mouth. The higher the port, the more severe the bit can be because it can also affect the roof of the horse's mouth. Some curb bits have copper rollers or "crickets" that encourage the horse to salivate and accept the bit.

The Pelham: This unjointed bit uses two reins and a curb chain. The top rein attaches to the big ring (the snaffle ring) on the cheekpiece. When you pull on this rein, the bit acts like a snaffle. The second rein fastens to the small bottom ring (the curb ring). When you pull on this rein, it puts pressure on the horse's mouth and poll. Pelhams have rubber or metal mouthpieces.

Holding two reins can be difficult, so many riders use a bit converter: a leather strap that attaches to both the snaffle and curb rings so you can use one rein. A bit converter makes a Pelham work like a strong snaffle.

A western curb bit has a raised part.

Pelham

GAG BITS

Gag bits raise up the head and are used on horses who put their heads down and take off with their riders. Once a horse's head is up, it's easier for a rider to stop her. Gag bits are very strong and should not be used by novices.

Some western riders use a full-cheek gag that looks similar to a curb bit. It can be jointed or unjointed. When the rein is pulled, the mouthpiece slides up the long cheekpieces and puts pressure on a horse's mouth. You may spot western gags in timed events in which a horse has to stop and turn quickly.

A western bosal hackamore is made of leather or rope.

Hackamores

Hackamores are bitless bridles used on horses who go better without a bitted bridle. A hackamore has reins attached to a noseband. When you pull on the reins, the noseband puts pressure on the horse's nose. A hackamore can cause pain and affect a horse's breathing, so use it gently.

A mechanical hackamore has a noseband with metal cheekpieces. It works like a curb bit, putting pressure on a horse's poll. A bosal hackamore has a noseband made of leather or rope, and it works by putting pressure on a horse's nose and jaw.

Nosebands

Nosebands are part of an English bridle, and there are different types, each with its own use. You may need to try a few before you find one that suits your horse. Here are a few popular nosebands:

Cavesson: This is the simplest noseband. It fastens below a horse's cheekbone and above the bit.

Dropped Noseband: This fastens in front of the bit and prevents a horse from opening her mouth and avoiding the bit. It can interfere with her breathing if not fitted properly. Only use it with a snaffle, never with a curb bit or gag.

Flash Noseband: This has a thin leather strap that threads through a loop on the front of the cavesson noseband, effectively creating two bands on the horse's face. The strap fastens below the bit and stops a horse from opening her mouth.

MARTINGALES
Martingales are leather straps that keep a horse from throwing her head up to avoid the bit. There are two kinds: running and standing.

This bridle features a flash noseband.

This horse is wearing a bridle with a figure-eight noseband and a running martingale.

Running Martingale: A running martingale has a leather strap that runs from the girth and divides into two thinner straps with metal rings on the ends. The reins are threaded through these rings. When your horse puts her head up high, a running martingale puts pressure on the bit though the reins.

A Standing Martingale or Western Tie-Down: This is a single leather strap that runs from the girth, between the forelegs, to the underside of the noseband. It is kept in place by a separate neck strap. Standing martingales and tie-downs put pressure on a horse's nose and are only used with a plain noseband. Often a tie-down or a standing martingale is fastened to a breastplate.

Breastplate or Western Breast Collar

Sometimes saddles move around or slip back. If a horse has low withers, for example, the saddle may slide from side to side. A breastplate/breast collar helps keep it secure.

A breastplate is a leather strap loosely worn across a horse's chest and attached to D-rings on the front of the saddle and the girth. They are often used by people who jump cross-country, such as eventers and hunting riders, or by people who trail ride through mountainous terrain.

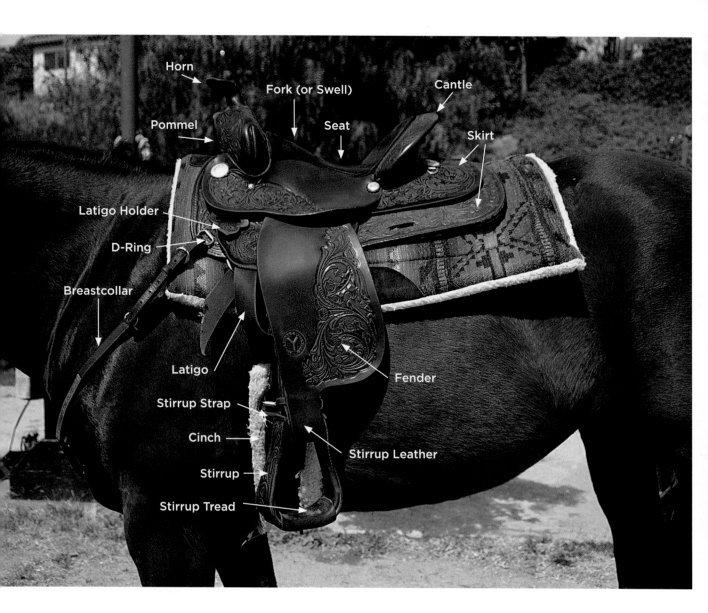

Horn

Pommel

Fork (or Swell)

Cantle

Seat

Skirt

Latigo Holder

D-Ring

Breastcollar

Latigo

Stirrup Strap

Cinch

Stirrup

Stirrup Tread

Fender

Stirrup Leather

WESTERN SADDLES

Western saddles are bigger and heavier than English saddles. They can weigh more than 30 pounds. They have wider seats for comfort on long rides. They spread a rider's weight more evenly on a horse's back than an English saddle.

The most distinguishing feature of the western saddle is the protruding horn in the front. Working cowboys and show or rodeo competitors use it to rope cows and horses.

The horn also comes in handy for new riders to hold onto in emergencies, but don't get into the habit of holding onto the horn. Not only will you look like a beginner, but it also throws off your balance. If you need extra stability, hold onto the cantle (back of the seat). Instead of pulling you forward, doing this will keep you deep in the seat.

Western saddles come in different styles:

General Purpose Saddle: The most commonly used western saddle is the general purpose saddle. It is popular with pleasure riders and folks who enjoy trail riding. It features a deep seat padded for extra comfort. It has a small horn because pleasure riders don't often rope calves!

Equitation Saddle: Designed for show, the leather is often elaborately decorated with embossing or hand-tooled designs. It is used in equitation classes and parades. The horn is fairly small. The seat is padded and is usually covered in suede to help the rider stay in the saddle.

Roping Saddle: A roping saddle is a heavy-duty saddle made of tough leather. The horn is large because riders use it to rope cows or store their coiled lassos. A roping saddle usually has a flat seat and a low cantle so a rider can hop in and out quickly and easily while he or she is working.

Saddle-Related Tack

SADDLE PAD

When you ride, a pad goes under your saddle to keep it clean and protect your horse's back. Saddle pads can be made of cotton, wool, fleece, felt, or foam. They are usually square or saddle-shaped, and come in a lot of colors—but white is used in the English show arena.

Western riders often use Navajo blankets—thick, rectangular pads made of wool or cotton. These colorful pads can be seen in the western show arena.

No matter what type of saddle pad you use, wash it regularly. A dirty pad rubs a horse and makes her uncomfortable. If you don't have access to a full-size washing machine, then try your local tack store. Some of them provide this laundering service.

GIRTH OR CINCH

A girth or a cinch is a belt that goes under your horse's belly and holds the saddle in place. English girths have two buckles at each end that attach to saddle girth straps, called "billets." English girths are usually made of leather, thick string, or synthetic materials such as nylon.

Western girths are called "cinches." They can be made of leather, mohair, cotton, wool, or synthetic materials. They have big rings at each end, one of which has a buckle tongue. Some western saddles use a rear cinch to help stabilize a saddle for roping.

STIRRUP LEATHERS

Used on English saddles, these long, buckled straps fasten to the saddle's stirrup bar and hold the stirrup irons. Stirrup leathers suffer a lot of stress, so check them for wear and tear regularly.

FENDERS

The fender is the western equivalent of a stirrup leather. The fender is a wide leather strap that connects the stirrup to the saddle.

STIRRUP IRONS AND TREADS

These are footrests that attach to the saddle with stirrup leathers. English stirrups are made of steel and should have rubber treads on them to keep your feet from slipping. Western stirrups are made of wood or synthetic materials covered in leather.

Boots and Bandages

Boots protect a horse's legs from knocks during such activities as jumping, barrel racing, and riding cross-country. Boots also help to support leg muscles because twisting a leg the wrong way—or knocking a jump—can pull, strain, or injure delicate tendons. Some horses, especially clumsy young ones or ones with poor conformation, kick themselves by mistake; in these instances, boots can help prevent injury.

Boots are made of leather or synthetic materials. They usually fasten by buckles or Velcro straps. The most commonly used boots are brushing boots, fetlock or ankle boots, and over-reach boots, also called "bell boots."

- Splint boots, sometimes called "brushing" boots, have padding that covers the inside of the leg and protects a horse if she hits the inside of one leg with the opposite hoof. They can be used on all four legs and cover the lower leg only.

- Fetlocks or ankle boots are a short version of the brushing boot and are used for the same purpose. They cover the fet-lock and heel area.

- Over-reach boots, or bell boots, belong on the front hooves. They fit around the pastern and protect the heels and coronet. Usually made of rubber and bell-shaped, they may fasten with buckles or Velcro, or simply pull over the

Tacking Up
a Horse

*t*acking up your horse seems complicated at first because there are a lot of confusing straps and buckles. Don't be afraid to ask for help.

If you take riding lessons, watch a groomer prepare your horse a few times; then ask to tack him up yourself. This is the best way to learn.

Carrying Tack

When you carry tack, it's best to hang the bridle over your shoulder. Rest an English saddle and pad on your forearm, and lay the girth over the saddle. Western riders grab the cantle with their right hand and hold on to the front of the saddle—not the horn—with their left.

If you must put a saddle on the ground, set it on its front end with the back end leaning against a wall or fence post. Drape the girth or cinch between the saddle and the wall so the saddle doesn't get scratched.

Tacking Up English Style

1 Fasten the pad to the saddle by its straps. Stand on your horse's left side and lightly place the saddle and pad in front of his withers (too far forward), then gently slide them back into their correct position. This keeps the horse's hair smooth under the saddle. Ruffled horse hair causes friction under the saddle, which can irritate your horse.

2 Walk around to your horse's right side with the girth, and attach it to the girth straps. Now, go to the left side, pull the girth underneath your horse's belly, and attach it to the two outside straps. Don't tighten it right away.

3 Make sure the saddle pad is pulled up into the gullet so it doesn't put pressure on your horse's spine.

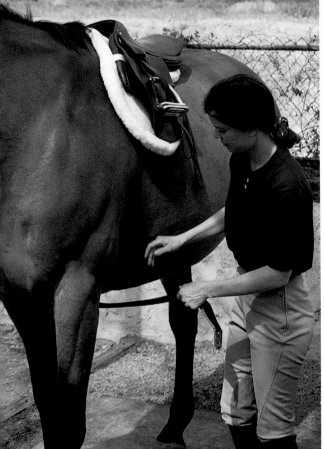

Slide an English saddle back into place (top left). Bring the girth up slowly so you don't *scare* your horse (bottom left) They stretch out the front legs so the girth doesn't pinch skin (above).

4 After you tighten the girth for the last time, and before you mount, stretch out your horse's forelegs to make sure the skin under the girth is smooth. Wrinkled skin causes sores.

5 Now, hold the bridle in front of your horse's head and slip the reins over his head, so you have some control when you take off the halter.

6 Stand next to your horse and take off his halter. Quickly slip your right hand under his neck and take hold of the bridle's cheekpieces. Your right hand should keep his head down. Put your left hand underneath the bit and bring it gently between his lips and up into his mouth. Your right hand should lift the bridle so the bit slips into place. Adjust the noseband so it's in the correct place and fasten it.

Put the reins over your horse's head first (below). Then, gently slide the bit into your horse's mouth (top right), and fasten the throatlatch last (bottom right).

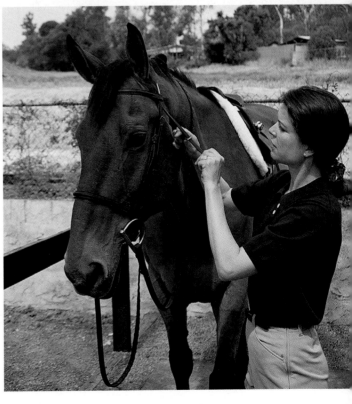

7 Once the bit is in place, hold the crown piece in your left hand. Use your right hand to gently bring his left ear, and then his right ear, under the crown piece. Straighten it out behind his ears, making sure the fit is as comfortable as possible and does not pull his ears.

8 Loosely fasten the throatlatch under his jaw. You should be able to fit four fingers between it and his throat for a comfortable fit.

9 Secure all the loose ends of straps in their leather keepers.

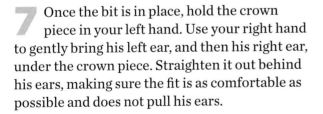

Tacking Up Western Style

1 Place the blanket on the horse's back, slightly forward, then slide it back into position. Make sure it hangs evenly on both sides of your horse.

2 Pick up the saddle by the horn, and then hold the front of the saddle with your left hand partially in the gullet. Your right hand can hold the back of the saddle. Place the right stirrup and cinch over the seat of the saddle so they don't bang your horse when you place the saddle on his back.

Stand on your horse's left side and swing the saddle into position on your horse's back. Do it swiftly but gently. Western saddles are heavy, and you may hurt your horse's back or scare him if you slam the saddle in place.

3 Walk around to the other side and lower the stirrups and cinch. Check that nothing is twisted. Release any saddle strings that might be stuck under the saddle. Return to the left side and make sure the saddle is sitting correctly. If it looks out of kilter, grab the horn and gently shake the saddle until it slips into place.

4 Stick a couple of fingers under the saddle pad right over the withers and lift it up a bit into the gullet.

5 Put up your left stirrup and reach underneath your horse for the cinch. Put the long latigo in your right hand and then run it down and up through the cinch ring. If the saddle is in the correct place, the cinch should be about 4 inches away from your horse's elbow. Then tighten the latigo. If you have a cinch with a buckle, simply buckle it to the latigo. If it is a traditional cinch without a buckle, tie the latigo to it with a knot.

Place the saddle onto your horse's back gently.

Do up the cinch slowly.

7 If you use a breastplate, put it on now. It shouldn't be so tight that it presses on your horse's windpipe.

8 Unbuckle your horse's halter and rebuckle it around his neck so he can't move off.

9 Stand next to your horse, facing the same direction. Hold the crown piece with your right hand and separate the bit from the curb chain with your left. Slip the bit into the horse's mouth. If your horse won't open his mouth, don't force it; you might end up hurting his gum or jaws. Sticking your thumb into the corner of his mouth may make him open up. Make sure your fingers don't get clamped in the horse's jaw.

6 If your saddle has a rear cinch, fasten it next. It shouldn't be as tight as the front one. Now connect the strap from the back cinch to the front cinch. Slip the excess latigo through the latigo holder.

10 As the bit slides in, raise the crown piece and carefully slide it over the left ear. Then, hold the crown piece in your left hand and use your right hand to slip his right ear under the crown piece or into its ear slot.

Carefully slide the crown piece over your horse's ears.

Does Your Tack Fit?

It's important that your tack fits your horse. If it's too big, it can rub and cause sores. If it's too small, it can pinch and make him uncomfortable. Here are some ways to make sure it fits properly:

- When you're in the saddle, you should be able to fit at least three fingers between the front of the saddle and the withers.

- The saddle's gullet should clear your horse's spine.

- If you have an English saddle, you should be able to fit three fingers between the cantle and your horse's back. If you have a western saddle, you should be able to fit three fingers between the back of the skirt and your horse's back.

- The stuffing or fleece on the bottom of the saddle should be smooth and without lumps so there is even pressure on your horse's back.

- Above the bit, there should be two or three wrinkles in the skin around the corner of your horse's mouth. If there are no wrinkles, the bit may be too low in his mouth.

- Now, check that the curb chain fits properly. You should be able to fit two fingers between the chain and your horse's chin.

- Make sure the western cinch rings are even on both sides of the horse.

Can you fit at least three fingers between the withers and the saddle?

Untacking English Style

1. First, take off the bridle. Unfasten the noseband and the throatlatch.

2. Slip the crown piece over your horse's ears with your right hand, and lower the bridle so that the bit comes out of his mouth. Do it slowly so the bit doesn't bang his teeth and chip or break them. The last thing you want to do is schedule a visit from the dentist. Keep the reins over his neck for control.

3. Put on your horse's halter and lead rope, then lift the reins over his head.

4. Run the irons up the leather until they are near the stirrup bars. Secure them by threading the rest of the leather through the stirrup.

5. Unbuckle the girth on the left side of your horse. Next, lift the saddle and pad off together. If the pad is damp, remove it and hang it up to dry.

Taking care of leather tack will make it last longer.

Cleaning Your Tack

Rinse off your bit after every ride, and clean your tack at least once a week. Saddlery is expensive, and it will last longer if you keep it clean. Dirty tack becomes stiff and breaks. When you clean your tack, check that the stitching isn't coming undone. If it's loose, take it to a tack shop for repair. To clean tack, you will need:

- a bucket of warm water
- leather dressing or saddle oil
- a piece of cloth or towel
- saddle soap
- two sponges

1 Take the bridle apart in pieces. Remove the stirrups and leathers from the saddle.

2 Dunk the bit in the bucket to soak. Then clean it off, rinse it, and leave it to dry. Your stirrups can go in the bucket next.

3 Dip one sponge in the water and wring it. It should be damp—not soaking wet. Use this sponge to clean your saddle and bridle, piece by piece.

4 When the leather is dry, put some saddle oil or dressing on a rag and work it into the areas of your tack that get used a lot, for example inside grooves and folds. Give the oil time to soak in.

5 Dampen the other sponge slightly. Rub or spray saddle soap on it and work it into the leather. Saddle soap gives your tack a protective coat and makes it shiny. Finally, take a cloth and polish your saddle and bridle.

Untacking Western Style

1 Take off the bridle first. Leave the reins over the horse's neck. Unfasten the throat-latch if there is one.

2 Bring the crown piece over the ears with your right hand, and slowly lower the bridle so the bit comes out of his mouth without banging his teeth. Put on his halter and lift the reins over his head.

3 If your saddle has a rear cinch, unfasten it first. Then unfasten the front cinch.

4 Secure the cinches and stirrups over the saddle so they don't swing.

5 Grab the front and back of the saddle, lift, and swing it off.

CHAPTER 8

Trailering a Horse

*i*f you plan to take your horse to shows, to other events, or on trail rides more than a few miles from home, you will have to load her into a trailer and drive there. But don't dash out and buy a trailer right away.

If you take lessons, your instructor may organize trailering for her students. She may get a big rig and share the costs or include them in the overall price of the outing. You might also find someone with a trailer who would like company going to horse events. Offer to share expenses and help pay for gas.

If you decide to buy a trailer, first make sure you have a vehicle that can pull it. Most experts recommend towing with a truck or utility vehicle that has a V-8 engine and a special towing package. Anything less and you will be under powered for towing.

What Kind of Trailer Do You Need?

Trailers come with either a ramp or a step-up entrance. Everyone has a preference. If you have no problems loading your horse, a step-up trailer may suit you fine, but some horses prefer getting in and out of a trailer using a ramp. Before you buy a trailer, try loading your horse into both types. Consider her reactions when

Try loading your horse in a step-up trailer before buying a new one.

Some horses find walking up a ramp easier than stepping into a trailer.

shop. Trailers with ramps tend to be heavier than the step-up types, so you must think about this if you have a small towing vehicle.

Some trailers carry the horses facing forward, side by side; others carry them at a slant. Slant trailers usually carry three or more horses. Many people feel that horses balance themselves better when they travel at an angle. Stock trailers are designed to carry all kinds of livestock, and are open on the inside (meaning no partitions). One type to avoid is the one-horse trailer. These can become unbalanced and tip over. Fortunately, few one-horse trailers exist today.

Some two-horse trailers have mangers with storage space underneath for tack. Those without storage space are called "walk-throughs" because you can lead your horse into the trailer, duck under a breast bar, and stand up again in an empty area. Most of these have small escape doors at the front. Some trailers have dressing rooms, too.

If you plan to do a lot of towing and have a big, tough truck, you could buy a gooseneck trailer. A gooseneck fastens to a hitch in the truckbed and balances its load over the back axle of the truck. Goosenecks give horses smoother rides than some other types of trailers.

American trailers generally come in four sizes: pony, quarter horse, Thoroughbred, and warmblood. Measure your horse before you shop. She needs plenty of headroom in her trailer.

Looking for a Trailer

If you have the money and want to buy a brand new trailer, check the Yellow Pages in your phone book, local horse magazines or on the Internet for a dealer. But if money is tight, look for a used trailer in the classified ads of a local horse magazine, newspaper or on the Internet. Here are some things to check before handing over any money for a used trailer:

Always put shipping boots on your horse's legs before a trip.

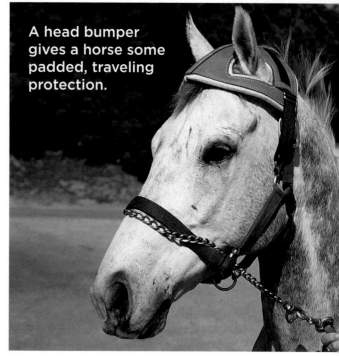

A head bumper gives a horse some padded, traveling protection.

Brakes: Most trailers have electrical brakes. Make sure they work!

Chains: These hold the trailer to the truck if the hitch comes undone.

Flooring: Lift up mats and look underneath the trailer to make sure the floor wood is strong, not rotting or weak.

Lights: Test all the lights.

Rust: If a trailer has a lot of rust, pass it by!

Tires, Ramp, Partition, and Axle: Check for wear and tear.

Windows: A trailer needs windows to provide ventilation.

Traveling Gear

Traveling in a trailer can be bumpy, so a horse should wear protective gear to prevent injuries. Here's what you need:

Head Bumper: If your horse throws her head around in a trailer, she should wear a head bumper. This is a padded hat with ear holes that attaches to the halter.

Shipping Bandages: Some people use bandages made of stretchy fabric instead of boots, but they must have some sort of padding under them or they won't offer protection. They take longer than boots to put on and remove.

Shipping Boots: These are padded boots that fasten easily with Velcro straps and are sold in sets of four. The best boots cover the knees and hooves of a horse's forelegs and the hocks and hooves of her hind legs. They are easy to put on and remove.

Tail Bandage: Some horses rub their tails on the back of the trailer. A stretchy tail bandage wraps around the top of a horse's tail and usually stops halfway down, where the tailbone ends.

For emergencies, always carry an extra halter and lead rope, plus a lead shank.

Drape the lead rope over your horse's neck when loading.

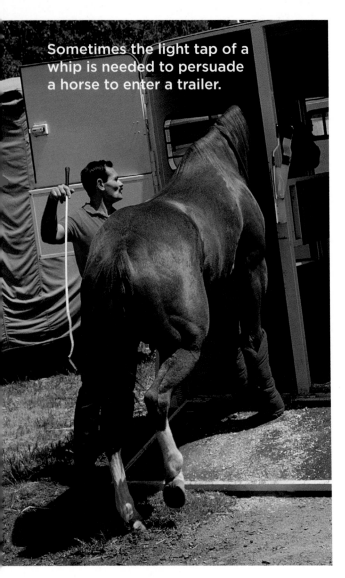

Sometimes the light tap of a whip is needed to persuade a horse to enter a trailer.

Loading a Horse

Before loading your horse, make the trailer as comfortable and pleasant as possible. Put straw or sawdust on the floor and make sure it's free of any slippery stuff, such as manure. Hang hay in a net or place it in the manger so your horse has something to nibble on during the journey. Open the escape doors, so the trailer is full of light and not so scary. Finally, lower the ramp or open the doors.

The way to load your horse depends on whether you have a walk-through or step-up trailer. Before loading either type of trailer, check that your horse's traveling boots or bandages are secure and that all straps are fastened properly. If your horse can be naughty, put a chain over her nose.

If you have a walk-through trailer or a big stock trailer with plenty of room and your horse is quiet and well behaved, you can lead her into the trailer. Walk next to her as you approach the trailer, then take a step or two in front of her. Walk briskly up the ramp or step. Your horse should follow. If you have a walk-through, you can duck under the breast bar so you don't get run over. Tie your horse to a piece of safety string attached to the tie-up ring.

If you have a step-up trailer or a horse who doesn't load easily, drape the lead rope over her neck and tie it to itself underneath, so it doesn't drag on the floor or get caught on something. Hold the lead rope a couple of inches under the horse's halter and walk along beside her, as you normally would. When you reach the trailer, turn so you are facing her shoulder. Give her a verbal signal or tap her gently with a long dressage crop or lunge whip on her hindquarters and ask her to move forward, as if she were on a lunge line. Let go of the lead rope. Give her a pat on her rear to reassure her as she steps up.

Once your horse is in the trailer, stand to one side and fasten the butt bar or chain as quickly as possible. Never stand directly behind her, in case she steps back and stomps on you by mistake. If the trailer has a ramp, lift it up, and secure the doors. Finally, walk to the front of the trailer, and tie your horse's lead rope to a safety string attached to a metal loop or a stretchy trailer tie.

Driving a Trailer

Driving a trailer takes practice, so go a few places without your horse first. You'll soon notice that it takes longer for your truck to stop and slow down when it's pulling a few thousand pounds.

It isn't easy for a horse to stay balanced in a trailer, so you must make stops gradually and go slow and wide around corners. If you zip sharply around bends, your horse could fall down. A horse will remember a bad ride, and you may have trouble loading her next time.

Unloading a Horse

Always untie your horse before unloading. If you are by yourself, open the escape door and drape the lead rope over her neck. Then head to the back of the trailer, open the door, and undo the butt bar or chain. Stand to one side and give your horse a verbal signal or gently tug on her tail to ask her to back out. Praise her when she steps out nicely. Grab hold of the lead rope.

TRAILERING TIPS

- Don't tie your horse too loose. She should not be able to reach over and nip at any companions.

- Always load a single horse on the left side, behind the driver. Roads are convex, with the highest part being in the middle. A trailer will stay better balanced if the horse is on the left. If you are towing two horses, put the heaviest on the left.

- Never get angry if you are having loading problems. Stay calm and don't upset your horse more. Ask a friend to walk behind your horse with a crop or lunge whip. He or she should give your horse a couple of light taps to make her go forward. If you are having serious problems, ask a trainer for some professional help.

- Clean out the trailer immediately after every journey. Urine and manure can soak through mats and ruin a floor.

- Make sure you always have a spare tire, a jack, and a lug wrench before you set off on a journey, and check your tire pressure frequently.

- If going in the trailer stresses your horse, feed her in it every once in

Always clean out the trailer after using it.

a while without driving anywhere, so she gets used to being in it.

A Caring Relationship

Now you should have a basic knowledge of what it takes to keep a horse in your care healthy and happy. You'll know when your horse is in good health and full of vigor. You'll be able to spot the warning signs that tell you that your horse is feeling under the weather, so you'll know when to call the veterinarian.

So, keep this book on a shelf in the barn. You may need to refer back to it from time to time. Now go out and spend some quality time with your horse!

Resources

**American Association
of Equine Practitioners**
4075 Iron Works Parkway
Lexington, KY 40511
859-233-0147
www.aaep.org

**American
Connemara
Pony Society**
P.O. Box 100
Middlebrook, VA 24450
540-866-2239
www.acps.org

American Driving Society
1837 Ludden Drive, Suite 120
Cross Plains, WI 53528
608-237-7382
www.americandrivingsociety.org

**American Endurance
Ride Conference**
P.O. 6027
Auburn, CA 95604
866-271-AERC (2372)
www.aerc.org

**American Farrier's
Association**
4059 Iron Works Parkway
Suite 1
Lexington, KY 40511
859-233-7411
www.theamericanfarriers.com

**American
Hanoverian Society**
4067 Iron Works Parkway
Suite 1
Lexington, KY 40511
859-255-4141
www.hanoverian.org

**American Holsteiner
Horse Association**
222 E. Main Street #1
Georgetown, KY 40324
502-863-4239
www.holsteiner.com

American Horse Council
1616 H Street N.W.
7th Floor
Washington, D.C. 20006
202-296-4031
www.horsecouncil.org

**American
Horse Protection
Association**
1000 29th Street
#T-100
Washington, D.C. 20007
202-965-0500

**American
Morgan Horse
Association**
122 Bostwick Road
Shelburne, VT 05482
802-985-4944
www.morganhorse.com

**American Mustang
and Burro
Association**
P.O. Box 608
Greeenwood, DE 19950
www.ambainc.net

**American Paint
Horse Association**
P.O. Box 961023
Fort Worth, TX 76161
817-834-APHA (2742)
www.apha.com

**American Quarter
Horse Association**
P.O. Box 200
Amarillo, TX 79168
806-376-4811
www.aqha.com

**American Riding
Instructors Association**
28801 Trenton Court
Bonita Springs, FL 34134
239-948-3232
www.riding-instructor.com

**American Saddlebred
Horse Association**
4083 Iron Works Parkway
Lexington, KY 40511
859-259-2742
www.asha.net

**American Society for the
Prevention of Cruelty to
Animals, National Animal
Poison Control Center**
424 E. 92nd Street
New York, NY 10128
*888-426-4435
www.aspca.org
*A $65 consultation fee may be
applied to your credit card.*

American Trails
P.O. Box 491797
Redding, CA 96049
530-547-2060
www.americantrails.org

**American Trakehner
Association**
1514 W. Church Street
Newark, OH 43055
740-344-1111
www.americantrakehner.com

**American
Warmblood Society**
2 Buffalo Run Road
Center Ridge, AR 72027
501-893-2777
www.americanwarmblood.org

**American Youth
Horse Council**
6660 #D-451 Delmonico
Colorado Springs, CO 80919
800-TRY-AYHC (897-2942)
www.ayhc.com

Appaloosa Horse Club Inc.
2720 W. Pullman Road
Moscow, ID 83843
208-882-5578
www.appaloosa.com

**Arabian Horse
Registry of America**
10805 E. Bethany Drive
Aurora, CO 80014
303-696-4500
www.arabianhorses.org

**California Department of Food
and Agriculture's Bureau of
Livestock Identification**
1220 N Street
Room A-130
Sacramento, CA 95814
916-654-0889
www.cdfa.ca.gov/ahfss/
livestock_ID

**Certified Horsmanship
Association**
4037 Iron Works Parkway,
Suite 180
Lexington, KY 40511
800-724-1446
www.cha-ahse.org

**Intercollegiate Horse
Show Association**
www.ihsainc.com

The Jockey Club
821 Corporate Drive
Lexington, KY 40503
859-224-2700
www.jockeyclub.com

**National Cutting
Horse Association**
260 Bailey Avenue
Fort Worth, TX 76107
817-244-6188
www.nchacutting.com

National 4-H Council
7100 Connecticut Avenue
Chevy Chase, MD 20815
301-961-2934
www.4-h.org

**National Western Stock
Show Association**
4655 Humboldt Street
Denver, CO 80216
303-297-1166
www.nationalwestern.com

**National Reining
Horse Association**
3000 N.W. 10th Street
Oklahoma City, OK 73107
405-946-7400
www.nrha.com

**North American
Riding for the
Handicapped Association**
P.O. Box 33150
Denver, CO 80233
800-369-RIDE (7433)
www.narha.org

**Palomino Horse
Breeders of America**
15253 E. Skelly Drive
Tulsa, OK 74116
www.palominohba.com

Performance Horse Registry
4047 Iron Works Parkway
Lexington, KY 40511
859-258-2472
www.phr.com

**Swedish Warmblood
Association of North America**
P.O. Box 788
Socorro, NM 87801
575-835-1318
www.wbstallions.com/wb/swana

**Tennessee Walking
Horse Breeders' and
Exhibitors' Association**
P.O. Box 286
Lewisburg, TN 37091
931-359-1574
www.twhbea.com

Trail Riders of Today
P.O. Box 30033
Bethesda, MD 20824
301-854-3467
www.trot-md.org

**United States
Dressage Federation**
4051 Iron Works Parkway
Lexington, KY 40511
859-971-2277
www.usdf.org

**United States
Equestrian Federation**
4047 Iron Works Parkway
Lexington, KY 40511
859-258-2472
www.usef.org

**The United States
Equestrian Team
Foundation**
P.O. Box 355
Gladstone, NJ 07934
908-234-1251
www.uset.org

**United States
Eventing Association**
525 Old Waterford Road N.W.
Leesburg, VA 20176
703-779-0440
www.eventingusa.com

**United States
Hunter Jumper
Association**
3870 Cigar Lane
Lexington, KY 40511
859-225-9033
www.ushja.org

**The United States
Pony Clubs**
4041 Iron Works Parkway
Lexington, KY 40511
859-254-7669
www.ponyclub.org

**United States
Team Penning
Association**
P.O. Box 4170
Fort Worth, TX 76164
817-378-8082
www.ustpa.com

Glossary

barrel racing: A timed contest in which a mounted rider makes sharp turns around three barrels set in a cloverleaf pattern.

bit: The mouthpiece on a bridle; there are many different types available.

bosal: A type of hackamore bridle with a simple noseband made of leather or rope attached to a large knot under the horse's chin.

breastplate: Also known as a breastband or breast collar; a device used across a horse's chest that attaches to the saddle and prevents slippage.

breeches: A pair of snug, stretchy English riding pants that cover the hips and thighs down to below the knee.

bridle: A head harness used to control and guide a horse.

bridle path: A section of mane on the top of a horse's head where the mane is trimmed to form a path for the halter or bridle to rest.

cantle: The rear part of a saddle that projects upward.

cinch: See girth.

crop: A short riding whip with a looped lash.

cross-country: A race that includes such events as timed hunter trials and chasing events, both of which are ridden at speed over natural fixed fences.

crown piece: A part of the bridle that goes over the horse's head and attaches to the cheekpiece.

curb bit: A bit with various mouthpieces and shanks, usually with a center rise that shifts pressure from the tongue to the roof of the mouth.

dressage: A form of exhibition riding in which the horse receives subtle, nearly invisible clues from the rider and performs a series of difficult steps and gaits with lightness of step and perfect balance. Dressage is also a classical training method that teaches the horse to be responsive, attentive, willing, and relaxed for the purpose of becoming a better equine athlete.

D-ring: A D-shaped metal fitting through which various parts of the harness pass.

endurance horse: A horse who competes in long-distance riding.

farrier: A person who shoes horses.

feed: Grain used for nourishment.

fetlock: A joint that makes a projection on the back of a horse's lower leg above the back of the hoof.

float: To file/rasp down the sharp edges on a horse's teeth.

frog: The triangular-shaped horny pad near the rear of the sole of a horse's foot.

girth: A band that encircles a horse's belly to hold a saddle on the horse's back.

gullet: In a western saddle, the open space under the horn.

hackamore: A type of bridle with a noseband that applies pressure on the nose for control instead of using a mouthpiece.

halter: A headpiece of leather, rope, or nylon used to lead a horse.

hand: A standard of equine height measurement derived from the width of a human hand. Each hand equals 4 inches, with fractions expressed in inches. A horse who is 16.2 hands is 16 hands, 2 inches, or 66 inches tall at the withers.

handling: Working with a horse while standing on the ground.

headstall: The pieces of a bridle, including the cheekstrap, throatlatch, crownpiece, browband, and noseband, if used.

horn: The projection above the raised part in the front of a western saddle.

jodhpurs: A style of riding pants that are close-fitting and cuffed at the ankle.

lameness: The condition of having a painful injury of the foot or leg that makes the horse limp or have an irregular gait.

lasso: A 30- to 40-foot-long rope with a running noose used for catching horses and cattle.

latigo: A strap that secures a girth to a saddle.

lead rope: A rope made out of cotton or nylon that can be clipped to a horse's halter.

martingale: A device for steadying a horse's head or maintaining proper head carriage.

muck heap: A pile located away from the stable where manure and soiled bedding are piled for removal.

muck out: To remove manure and soiled bedding from a horse's living area.

noseband: Part of an English bridle comprising a strap that goes over the nose.

open rein: A training action of holding a rein in each hand and directing a turn by holding one rein toward the rider's knee in the direction of the turn.

pommel: The raised part of the front of a saddle.

pulling the mane: Thinning the hair in the mane by pulling part of the hair out; this can also be done to thin the tail.

purebred: A horse of a distinct breed whose parents are registered in the same studbook without a mixture of breeds.

sheath: The organ that encases an unextended penis.

show jumpers: People and horses who compete in show jumping.

show jumping: The competitive riding of horses over a course of obstacles, judging on ability and speed.

snaffle: A type of mild bit.

splints: A condition in which a bony growth forms on the horse's cannon bone (lower leg). Tearing of a ligament between the cannon bone and a neighboring splint bone causes a hot, painful swelling and the formation of a splint.

split reins: Western-style reins that do not join at their ends.

tack: Saddle, bridle, and other equipment used in riding and handling a horse.

three-day eventer: A horse who competes in a competition that continues over three days and includes a dressage test, a cross-country event, and show jumping.

throatlatch: A bridle strap that goes under the horse's throat.

tree (saddle tree): The frame of a saddle.

withers: The highest part of a horse's back, where the neck and the back join.